Thomas Camp

J. Cuthbert Hadden

Alpha Editions

This edition published in 2023

ISBN : 9789357941334

Design and Setting By
Alpha Editions
www.alphaedis.com
Email - info@alphaedis.com

Contents

PREFACE ....- 1 -

CHAPTER I ANCESTRY—BIRTH—SCHOOLDAYS ....- 2 -

CHAPTER II COLLEGE AND HIGHLAND
TUTORSHIPS ....- 9 -

CHAPTER III 'THE PLEASURES OF HOPE' ....- 19 -

CHAPTER IV CONTINENTAL TRAVELS ....- 29 -

CHAPTER V WANDERINGS—MARRIAGE—
SETTLEMENT IN LONDON...- 39 -

CHAPTER VI POETICAL WORK AND PROSE
BOOKMAKING..- 51 -

CHAPTER VII LECTURES AND TRAVELS ....- 60 -

CHAPTER VIII CLOSING YEARS ....- 75 -

CHAPTER IX PERSONAL CHARACTERISTICS AND
PLACE AS A POET..- 87 -

FOOTNOTES ....- 97 -

PREFACE

Reviewing Beattie's Life of Campbell in the *Quarterly* in 1849, Lockhart expressed the hope that no one would ever tell Campbell's story without making due acknowledgment to 'the best stay of his declining period.' He would be a bold man who would think of doing so. As well might one expect to write a life of Johnson without the aid of Boswell as expect to tell Campbell's story without reference to Dr Beattie. In addition to my acknowledgments to him, I have to express my indebtedness to Mr Cyrus Redding's 'Reminiscences of Thomas Campbell,' which, though badly put together, yet contain a mass of valuable information about the poet, especially in his more intimate relations. For the rest I have made considerable use of Campbell's correspondence, and have, I trust, acquainted myself with all the more important references made to him in contemporary records, and in the writings of those who knew him. To several of my personal friends, particularly to Mr G. H. Ely, I am obliged for hints and helpful suggestions, which I gratefully acknowledge.

J. C. H.

EDINBURGH, *October 1899.*

CHAPTER I
ANCESTRY—BIRTH—SCHOOLDAYS

The Campbells, as everybody knows, can claim an incredibly long descent. There is a Clan Campbell Society, the chairman of which declared some years ago that he possessed a pedigree carrying the family back to the year 420, and no doubt there are enthusiasts who can trace it to at least the time of the Flood. The poet was not particular about his pedigree, but the biographer of a Campbell would be doing less than justice to his subject if he denied him that ell of genealogy which Lockhart deemed the due of every man who glories in being a Scot.

In the present case, fortunately for the biographer, there is authoritative assistance at hand. The poet's uncle, Robert Campbell, a political writer under Walpole's administration, made a special study of the genealogy of the Campbells; and in his 'Life of the most illustrious Prince John, Duke of Argyll,' he has traced for us the descent of that particular branch of the Clan to which the poet's family belonged. The descent may be stated in a few words. Archibald Campbell, lord and knight of Lochawe, was grandson of Sir Neil, Chief of the Clan, and a celebrated contemporary of Robert the Bruce. He died in 1360, leaving three sons, from one of whom, Iver, sprang the Campbells in whom we are now interested. They were known as the Campbells of Kirnan, an estate lying in the pastoral vale of Glassary, in Argyllshire, with which, through many generations, they became identified as lairds and heritors, 'supporters of the Reformation and elders in the Church.' In a privately printed work dealing with the Clan Iver, the late Principal Campbell of Aberdeen, who was distantly related to the poet, gives a slightly different account of the origin of the Kirnan Campbells, but the matter need not be dwelt upon here. There is a suggestion, scouted by Principal Campbell, that the poet believed himself to be remotely connected with the great ducal house of Argyll. In some lines written 'On receiving a Seal with the Campbell Crest,' he speaks of himself as having been blown, a scattered leaf from the feudal tree, 'in Fortune's mutability'; and even Lady Charlotte Campbell, a daughter of the 'illustrious Prince John,' hails him as a clansman of her race, exclaiming 'How proudly do I call thee one of mine!'

These, however, are speculations for the antiquary rather than for the biographer. They are interesting enough in their way, but the writer of a small volume like the present cannot afford to be discursive; and so, leaving the arid regions of genealogy, we may be content to begin with the poet's grandfather, Archibald Campbell. He was the last to reside on the family estate of Kirnan. Late in life he had taken a second wife, a daughter of Stewart, the laird of Ascog. Before her marriage the lady had lived much in the Lowlands, and now she said she could not live in the Highlands: the solitude preyed upon her health and spirits. Hence it came about that the laird of Kirnan set up house in an old mansion in the Trunkmaker's Row, off the Canongate of Edinburgh, where the poet's father, the youngest of three sons, was born in 1710.

Beyond the interesting fact that he was educated under the care of Robert Wodrow, the celebrated historian and preacher, from whose teaching he drew the strict religious principles which regulated his life, we hear nothing of the earlier years of Alexander Campbell. He went to America, and was in business for some time at Falmouth, in Virginia. There he met with the son of a Glasgow merchant, another Campbell, to whom he was quite unrelated, and together the two returned to Scotland to start in Glasgow as Virginia traders. The new firm at first prospered in a high degree, for Glasgow about the middle of the eighteenth century was just touching the culminating point of her commerce with the American colonies. Even as early as 1735 the Glasgow merchants had fifteen large vessels engaged in the tobacco trade alone. But the outbreak of the American War in 1775 put a speedy end to the city's success in this direction. 'Some of the Virginia lords,' says Dr Strang, 'ere long retired from the trade, and others of them were ultimately ruined. Business for a time was in fact paralysed, and a universal cry of distress was heard throughout the town.'

Of course the Campbell firm suffered with the rest. Beattie, who had access to the books, declares that Alexander Campbell's personal loss could not have been less than twenty thousand pounds. Whatever the sum was, it represented practically the whole of Campbell's savings. This was a serious blow to a man of sixty-five, with ten surviving children and an eleventh child expected. He set himself to retrieve his fortunes as best he could, but he never recovered his position; and we are told that his family henceforward had to be brought up on an income—partly derived from boarders—that barely sufficed to purchase the common necessaries of life. It was, however, in these days of declining fortunes that the family was destined to receive its most notable member. The eleventh and last child, anticipated perhaps with misgiving, was Thomas Campbell, who was born on the 27th of July 1777, his father being then sixty-seven, and his mother some twenty-five years less.[1]

It will be well to say here all that needs farther to be said about the poet's parents. Alexander Campbell belonged to a Scottish type now all but extinct—stolid, meditative, somewhat dour, fond of theology and the abstract sciences: leading the family devotions in extempore prayer; regarding the Sunday sermon as essential to salvation, and less concerned about the amount of his income than about his honour and integrity. As his son puts it:

> Truth, standing on her solid square, from youth
>
> He worshipped—stern, uncompromising truth.

That he was a man of character and intelligence is clear from the fact that he numbered among his intimates such distinguished men as Adam Smith and Dr Thomas Reid, the successive occupants of the Moral Philosophy Chair at Glasgow. When Reid published his 'Inquiry into the Human Mind,' he gave a copy to Alexander Campbell, who read it and said he was edified by it. 'I am glad you are pleased with it,' remarked Reid; 'there are now at least two men in Glasgow who understand my work—Alexander Campbell and myself.' He had the saving grace of humour, too, this old Virginia trader, though, from a specimen given, it was apparently not of a very brilliant kind. Some of the boys were discussing the best colours for a new suit of clothes. 'Lads,' said the father, whose propensity for punning not even chagrin at the law's delays could suppress, 'lads, if you wish to get a lasting suit, get one like mine. I have a suit in the Court of Chancery which has lasted thirty years, and I think it will never wear out.' The worthy man lived to the patriarchal age of ninety-one, dying in Edinburgh—whither he had retired with his household three years before—in 1801. In his last days 'my son Thomas' was the main theme of his conversation.

Alexander Campbell had not married until he reached his forty-sixth year, and then he chose the young sister of his partner, an energetic girl of twenty-one. It must have been from her that the son drew his poetic strain. She is spoken of as 'an admirable manager and a clever woman,' and, what is of more interest, 'a person of much taste and refinement.' She brought to the home the poetry in counterpoise to her husband's philosophy. Like Leigh Hunt's mother, she was 'fond of music, and a gentle singer in her way': her poet son, as we shall find, was also fond of music, sang a little, and was, in his earlier years at least, devoted to the flute. To her children she was certainly not over-indulgent; indeed she is said to have been 'unnecessarily severe or even harsh'; but the mother of so large a family, with ordinary cares enhanced by the necessity for practising petty economies, would have been an angel if she had always been sweet and gracious. Between her and her youngest boy there seems to have been a particular affection, and when he began to make some stir in the world, no one was more elated with pardonable pride than she. There is a story told of her having asked a shopman to address a parcel to 'Mrs Campbell, mother of the author of "The Pleasures of Hope."' She survived her husband for eleven years, and died in Edinburgh in 1812, at the age of seventy-six.

The house in which Campbell and his family resided at the time of the poet's birth, was a little to the west of High Street near the foot of Balmanno Brae, and in the line of the present George Street. Beattie, writing in 1849, speaks of it as having long since disappeared under the march of civic improvement, and as a matter of fact it was demolished in 1794 when George Street was opened up. The Glasgow of 1777 was of course a very different place from what it is to-day—very different from what it was when Defoe could describe it as 'one of the cleanest, most beautiful, and best-built cities of Great Britain'; when Smollett, himself a Glasgow youth, saw in it 'one of the prettiest towns in Europe.' In 1777 Glasgow was only laying the foundations of her commercial prosperity. She had, it is true, established her tobacco trade with the American plantations, and her sugar trade with the West Indies, but her character as the seat of an ancient Church and University had not been materially altered thereby.

Even in 1773, when Johnson, on his way back from the Hebrides, had a look round her sights, he found learning 'an object of wide importance, and the habit of application much more general than in the neighbouring University of Edinburgh.' Trade and letters still joined hands, so that Gibbon could not inappropriately speak of Glasgow as 'the literary and commercial city,' and one might still walk her streets without at every corner being 'nosed,' to use De Quincey's phrase, by something which reminded him of 'that detestable commerce.' Whether Glasgow was altogether a meet nurse for a poetic child may perhaps be doubted. The time came when Campbell himself thought she was not. The town, said he, has 'a cold, raw, wretchedly wet climate, the very nursery of sore throats and chest diseases.' Redding once chaffed him about it. 'Did you ever see Wapping on a drizzling, wet, spring day?' he asked in reply. 'That is just the appearance of Glasgow for three parts of the year.' But Glasgow was not so bad as yet. She was still surrounded by the cornfields and the hedgerows and the orchards of Lanarkshire, her few streets practically within a stone's throw of the Cathedral and the College.

The youngest of their family, the son of the father's old age, Thomas Campbell was naturally thought much of by his parents. He had been baptized by, and indeed named after, Dr Thomas Reid, and the old Virginia merchant is said to have had a presentiment that he would in some way or other do honour to his name and country. What proud father has not thought the same? That he was regarded as a precocious child goes without saying. We are told that he uttered quaint, old-fashioned remarks which were 'much too wise for his little curly head'; and he was of so inquisitive a turn—but then all children are inquisitive—that he found amusement and information in everything that fell in his way. A sister, nineteen years his senior, taught him his letters; and in 1785 he was handed over to the care of David Allison, the scholarly master of the Grammar School. Allison was a rigid disciplinarian of the good old type, who seems to have whipped the dead languages into his pupils with all the energy of Gil Blas' master. Campbell remained under him for four years. He began his studies in such earnest that he made himself ill, and had to be removed to a cottage at Cathcart, where for six weeks he was nursed by an aged 'webster' and his wife.

No doubt the little holiday had its influence at the time; it certainly had its influence in later life when, after a visit to the 'green waving woods on the margin of Cart,' he wrote his not unpleasing stanzas on this scene of his early youth. In any case he left the country cottage rather reluctantly, and returned to his lessons at the Grammar School. He does not appear to have been a particularly industrious student. He had certainly an ambition to excel, and he was invariably at the top of his class; but he made progress rather by fits and starts than by steady, laborious plodding. In this respect, of course, he was only like a great many more celebrities who have been dunces in the schoolroom. Not that Campbell was in any sense a dunce. He was especially enamoured of the classics; so much so, indeed, that, as Beattie gravely certifies, he 'could declaim with great fluency at the evening fireside in the language of Greece and Rome'; and some of the translations which he made for Allison were considered good enough to be printed by the enthusiastic biographer. His love for Greek, in particular, was the subject of much remark, both then and afterwards. Redding says he could repeat thirty or forty Greek verses applicable to any subject that might be under discussion. Beattie, again, tells that Greek was his 'pride and solace' all through life; and there is good authority for saying that, even after he had made a name as a poet, he wished to be considered a Greek scholar first and a poet afterwards. That he was quite sincere in the matter may be gathered from the circumstance of his having in his last days given his niece a series of daily lessons in the language of Homer, 'all in the Greek character and written with his own hand.' Nevertheless, as a Grecian, the classical world can as well do without Thomas Campbell as the Principal at Louvain, in 'The Vicar of Wakefield,' found that he could do without Greek itself.

With all his enthusiasm for the classics, Campbell does not seem to have been anything less of a boy than his fellows at the Grammar School. He loved Greek, but he loved games too. There are tales of stone fights with the Shettleston urchins, such as Scott has described in his story of Green-breeks, and of strawberry raids in suburban gardens which for days afterwards made him restive under the pious literature prescribed by his father. That he was indeed a very boy is shown by at least one amusing anecdote. His mother had a cousin, an old bedridden lady, about whose frail tenure of life she felt much anxiety. Every morning she would send either Tom or his brother Daniel to ask 'how Mrs Simpson was to-day.' One day Tom wanted to go on a blackberry expedition; his mother wanted him to inquire, as usual, about 'this deil of an auld wife that would neither die nor get better.' Daniel suggested that there was no need to go: 'just say that she's better or worse.' The boys continued to report in this way for weeks and months, but finding that an unfavourable bulletin only sent them back earlier next morning, they agreed that the old lady should get better. One day Tom announced that Mrs Simpson had quite recovered—and a few hours later the funeral invitation arrived! Campbell, in telling the story long after, says he was much less pained by the cuffing he received from his mother than by a few words from his father. The old man 'never raised a hand to us, and I would advise all fathers who would have their children to love their memory to follow his example.' The wisdom is not Solomonic, but that Campbell set much store by it is quite evident from the frequent reference which he makes in later life to his father's sparing of the rod.

Meanwhile he was giving indication of his literary bent in the manner usual with youngsters. The 'magic of nature,' to quote his own words, had first 'breathed on his mind' during his six weeks in the country, and the result was a 'Poem on the Seasons,' in which the conventional expression of the obvious runs through some hundred lines or more. A year later, that is to say in 1788, he wrote an elegy 'On the death of a favourite parrot,' of which one can only remark that it will at least bear comparison with the reputed tribute of Master Samuel Johnson to his duck. Strange to say among the last things which Campbell wrote were some lines on a parrot, so that any one who is interested enough can make a critical comparison between his elegiac poems in youth and age.

But Campbell was doing better things than calling upon Melpomene, the queen of tears, to attend his 'dirge of woe' on account of poor Poll. Mr Allison was in the habit of prescribing translations from the classics into English, which might be either in prose or in verse, as his pupils thought fit. Campbell chose verse. He made translations from Anacreon, from Virgil, from Horace, and from other Greek and Latin writers, all with a fair measure of success, considering his years. Indeed these verse translations are much superior to his original efforts of the same and even of later date. Beattie, who saw the manuscripts, remarked upon the almost total absence of punctuation in them all. It seems that Campbell regarded the art of pointing as one of the mysteries, to which for many years he paid as little attention as if he had been an eighteenth century lawyer's clerk. Even as late as 'Theodoric' (1824), he had to ask a literary friend to look after the punctuation in the proofs.

There was, however, no printer's convenience to study in these early days; and the verse translations, punctuated or not, served their purpose, not only in bringing prizes to the young student, but in contributing towards the acquirement of that facility in verse-making which helped to lay the foundation of his future fame. The provoking thing was that his father did not approve of making verses. Like Jack Lofty, he thought poetry 'a pretty thing enough' for one's wives and daughters, but not for men who have to make their living in the world; and he would much rather have seen his son writing in the sober prose of his beloved Doddridge and Sherlock than after the manner of Dryden and Pope. 'Many a sheet of nonsense have I beside me,' wrote Campbell in 1794, 'insomuch that when my father comes into my room, he tells me I would be much better reading Locke than scribbling so.' But Campbell believed that he had been born a poet, and although he did not entirely ignore his father's favourites, he kept thumbing his Milton and other models, and informed the parent—actually in verse too!—that while philosophers and sages are not without their influence on the stream of life, it is after all the poet who

Refines its fountain springs,

The nobler passions of the soul.

CHAPTER II
COLLEGE AND HIGHLAND TUTORSHIPS

When Campbell said farewell to the Grammar School prior to entering his name at College, it was observed of him that no boy of his age had ever left more esteemed by his classfellows or with better prospects at the University. His first College session began in October 1791. At that time the University was located in the High Street, the classic Molendinar, as yet uncovered, finding a way to the Clyde through its park and gardens. Johnson thought it was 'without a sufficient share in the magnificence of the place'; and not unlikely the scarlet gowns worn by the students were in Campbell's day pretty much what they were when Wesley reported them 'very dirty, some very ragged, and all of coarse cloth.' But there must have been something very pleasant about the quaint old world life which was then lived in and around the College Squares. Close upon four hundred students used to gather about the time-honoured courts, the windows of the professors' houses looking down upon them from the north side; and the memories of many generations must have gone some little way to atone for the lack of 'magnificence' so much deplored by the great Cham of literature.

The list of professors in 1791, when Campbell entered, did not include any name of outstanding note. His father's old friend, Dr Reid, now a veteran of eighty-one, had retired, though he was still living in the Professors' Court, and had been succeeded by Professor Arthur, a scholar of respectable ability and varied acquirements, for whom Campbell expressed a sincere admiration. The Greek class was taught by Professor Young, a character of the Christopher North and John Stuart Blackie type, 'a strangely beautiful and radiant figure in the then grave and solemn group of Glasgow professors.' William Richardson filled the Humanity—in other words the Latin—Chair, and filled it with some distinction too, in his curled wig, lace ruffles, knee breeches and silk stockings. Richardson was not of those who combine plain living with high thinking. Dining out was his passion. It is told of him that one evening, when the turtle soup was unusually fine, he exclaimed, after repeated helpings, 'I know there is gout in every spoonful, but I can't resist it.' For all this, he was a good scholar and an expert teacher, enjoying some repute as one of Mackenzie's coadjutors in *The Mirror*; a poet, too, and the author of one or two books which were read in their day. The Logic class was in the hands of Professor Jardine, 'the philosophic Jardine,' as Campbell calls him—'a most worthy, honest man, neither proud nor partial.' Campbell says he could not boast of deriving any great advantage from Jardine's class, but he 'found its employment very agreeable' nevertheless, and he seems to have honestly liked the professor. The Law Chair was occupied by Professor Millar, a violent democrat, who, in the dark days of Toryism, 'did much in Glasgow to inoculate Jeffrey and the academic Liberals with zealous views of progress.' Campbell regarded him as the ablest of all the professors; and although he was not a regular student of law, he attended some of the lectures, and was inclined to credit Millar with influencing his views on what he termed the ascendency of freedom.

Such were the men under whose direction the poet completed his education. Of fellow-students with whom he was intimate it is not necessary to say much. Perhaps the best known was Hamilton Paul, a jovial youth with a talent for verse, who afterwards, when minister of Broughton, narrowly escaped censure from the Church courts for an attempt to palliate the shortcomings of Burns by indiscreet allusions to his own clerical brethren. Paul and Campbell were frequently rivals in competing for academical rewards offered for the best compositions in verse, and in one case at least Campbell was beaten. It was Paul who founded the College Debating Club, which usually met in his lodgings and occasionally continued its debates till midnight; and in some published recollections of the Club's doings he bears testimony to Campbell's great fluency as a speaker. Another fellow-student was Gregory Watt, a son of the famous engineer. Campbell described him as 'unparalleled in his early talent for eloquence,' as literally the most beautiful youth he had ever seen; and he declared afterwards that if Watt had lived he must have made a brilliant figure in the House of Commons. Then there was James Thomson, a kindred genius, known familiarly as the 'Doctor,' with whom he formed a life-long friendship, and to whom some of the most intimate of his letters are addressed. It was to the order of this early friend that two marble busts of the poet were executed by Bailey, one of which he presented to Glasgow University; and it was he who also commissioned the well-known portrait by Sir Thomas Lawrence, which accompanies most editions of Campbell's works. Unfortunately, Campbell just missed Jeffrey, the 'great little man,' who spent two happy years (1788-1790) at the old College, and, like Campbell himself, was subsequently made its Lord Rector.

Campbell's career at the University, allowing for certain differences of detail, was very much what it had been at the Grammar School. That is to say, he fought shy of drudgery, put on a spurt now and again, distinguished himself in the classics, wrote verse, and indulged freely in the customary frolics of the typical student. He confessed in after life that he was much more inclined to sport than study; and although he admitted having carried away one or two prizes, he admitted also that he was idle in some of the classes. The fact remains notwithstanding, that he constantly outstripped his competitors, who, as Beattie has it, steadily plodded on in the rear, 'the very personifications of industry.' In his first year he took one prize for Latin and another for some English verses, besides securing a bursary on Archbishop Leighton's foundation. Next session he had more academical honours. In the

Logic class he received the eighth prize for 'the best composition on various subjects,' and was made an examiner of the exercises sent in by the other students of the class—certainly a high compliment to a youth of his years. One of the essays, on the subject of Sympathy, is printed by Beattie with the Professor's note appended. From this note it appears that the occult art of pointing was not the only matter which required the attention of the student. Professor Jardine might have passed over the amazing statement that 'God has implanted in our nature an emotion of pleasure on contemplating the sufferings of a fellow-creature'; but it was impossible that he should overlook such spellings as 'agreable,' 'sympathyze,' and 'persuits.' Still, 'upon the whole,' said Jardine, 'the exercise is good, and entitles the author to much commendation.'

The Professor's verdict may be taken as a type of Campbell's whole career at College: it was a case of 'much commendation' all through. At the close of his third session he was awarded a prize for a poetical 'Essay on the Origin of Evil,' which, if we are to credit his own statement, gave him a celebrity throughout the entire city, from the High Church down to the bottom of the Saltmarket. The students, who spoke of him as the Pope of Glasgow, even talked of it over their oysters at Lucky MacAlpine's in the Trongate. In the Greek class he took the first prize for a rendering of certain passages from the 'Clouds' of Aristophanes, which Professor Young declared to be the best essay that had ever been given in by a student at the University. This was not bad for a youth of fifteen. Hamilton Paul says that Campbell carried everything before him in the matter of his 'unrivalled translations,' until his fellow-students began to regard him as a prodigy, and copy him as a model. In Galt's Autobiography there is a story—he heads it 'A Twopenny Effusion'—to the effect that the students bore the cost of printing an Ossianic poem of Campbell's which was hawked about at twopence; but as Galt erroneously says that Campbell published 'The Pleasures of Hope' by subscription, we may regard the story as at least doubtful. Campbell called Galt a 'dirty blackguard' for retailing it.

But it was not alone by his proficiency in the classics that Campbell compelled attention. At this time he showed a turn for satire, of which he never afterwards gave much evidence, and his lampoons upon characters in the College and elsewhere were the theme of constant merriment in the quadrangle. Beattie has a good deal to say about these effusions, but if we may judge by a sample which Redding has preserved, their cleverness was better than their taste. It was legitimate enough, perhaps, to rail at the length of an elderly city parson's sermons, to make fun of his oft-recurring phrase, 'the good old-way'; but the worthy man, about to marry a young wife, could hardly be expected to relish this kind of thing:

So for another Shunamite

He hunts the city day by day,

To warm his chilly veins at night

In the good old way.

Adam Smith contended that it was the duty of a poet to write like a gentleman. If as a student Campbell had always written like a gentleman, there would have been less of that posthumous resentment of which his biographer complains. Nevertheless, his popularity as a playful wit must have been very pleasant to him at the time. 'What's Tom Campbell been saying?' was a common exclamation among the students as they gathered of mornings round the stove in the Logic classroom. And Tom Campbell, if he had been saying nothing of particular note, would take his pencil and write an impromptu on the white-washed wall. Presently a ring would be formed round it, 'and the wit and words passing from lip to lip generally threw the class into a roar of laughter.' It is but right to say, however, that these impromptus were invariably produced with a view to something else than praise. The stove was usually encircled by a body of stout, rollicking Irish students, and Campbell found that the only sure means of getting near it was by 'drafting the fire-worshippers'—in other words, by making them give warmth in exchange for wit. One cold December morning it was whispered that a libel on old Ireland had been perpetrated on the wall. The Irishmen rushed forth in a body, and while they read, *apropos* of a passage they had just been studying in the class—

Vos, Hiberni, collocatis,

Summum bonum in—potatoes,

the young satirist had taken the best place at the stove!

Campbell's third session at the University was eventful in several respects. To begin with, it was then—in the spring of 1793—that he made that first visit to Edinburgh to which he so often referred afterwards. It was a time of intense political excitement. 'The French Revolution,' to quote the poet's words, 'had everywhere lighted up the contending spirits of democracy and aristocracy'; and being, in his own estimation, a competent judge of politics, Campbell became a pronounced democrat. Muir and Gerald were about to stand their trial for high treason at Edinburgh, and Campbell 'longed insufferably' to see them—to see Muir especially, of whose accomplishments he had heard a 'magnificent account.' He had an aunt in Edinburgh ready to welcome him; and so, with a crown piece in his pocket, he started for the capital, doing the forty-two miles on foot. Next morning found him in court. The trial was, he says, an era in his life. 'Hitherto I had never known what public eloquence was, and I am sure the Justiciary Scotch lords did not help me to a conception of it, speaking, as they did, bad arguments in broad Scotch. But the Lord Advocate's speech was good—the speeches of Laing and Gillies were better; and Gerald's speech annihilated the remembrances of all the eloquence that had ever been heard within the walls of that house.' In the opinion of eminent English lawyers Gerald had not really been guilty of sedition, and certainly Muir never uttered a sentence in favour of reform stronger than Pitt himself had uttered. Nevertheless, in spite of their solemn protests and their fervent appeals to the jury, they were both sentenced to transportation, and were sent in irons to the hulks.

The trial and its sequel made a deep impression on the young democrat. When he returned to Glasgow he could think and speak of nothing else. His old gaiety had quite deserted him, and instead of frolics and flute-playing and 'auld farrant stories' by the fireside, there were tirades about 'the miserable prospects of society, the corrupt state of modern legislature, the glory of ancient republics, and the wisdom of Solon and Lycurgus.' Never, surely, was any philosopher of fifteen so harassed by political cares and apprehensions. But the gloomy fit did not last long. Campbell had to think of making a living for himself, and he began by casting about for something to fill up his college vacations.

It does not appear that he went to the University with any definite object in view, but the question of a profession had long since become a pressing consideration. Naturally he looked first towards the Church, but his father, unlike the majority of Scots parents about that time, did not encourage him in the notion of wagging his head in a pulpit; and so, after toying with theology—he studied Hebrew and wrote a hymn—he turned his attention in other directions. He thought of law, and spent some time in the office of a city solicitor. Then he thought of business, and filled up a summer recess in the counting-house of a Glasgow merchant, 'busily employed at book-keeping and endeavouring to improve this hand of mine.' Next he tried medicine, but had to give it up because he could not bear to witness the surgical operations. Finally he fell back on the last resource of the University man without a profession, and became a tutor. According to Dr Holmes, the natural end of the tutor is to die of starvation. Campbell's dread was that he would die of dulness: he had engaged to go to the farthest end of the Isle of Mull—

Where the Atlantic wave

Pours in among the stormy Hebrides.

It turned out to be not quite so bad as he anticipated, though, in truth, the reality proved much less pleasant than the retrospect. In the meantime he had a very sprightly journey from Glasgow in the company of Joseph Finlayson, an old classfellow who was also going to taste the bitterness of a Highland tutorship. The pair started on the 18th of May 1795. At Greenock they spent a long evening on the quay, 'for economy's sake,' and distinguished themselves by saving a boy from drowning. Campbell thought it pretty hard that two such heroes should go supperless to bed; so they repaired to the inn, ate—according to their own account—dish after dish of beefsteaks, and drank tankards of ale that set them both singing and reciting poetry like mad minstrels of the olden time. Next day, leaving their trunks to be sent by land to Inverary, they crossed the Firth of Clyde to Argyllshire, the jolliest boys in the whole world. Campbell says he had still a half-belief in Ossian, and an Ossianic interest in the Gaelic people; but this did not reconcile him to the Highland beds, in which 'it was not safe to lay yourself down without being troubled with cutaneous sensations next morning.' Nor did the bill of fare at the Highland inns please the travellers any better. It lacked variety. Everywhere it was 'Skatan agas, spuntat agas, usquebaugh'—herrings and potatoes and whisky. But the roaring streams, and the primroses, and the 'chanting cuckoos' made up for all the discomfort. Campbell, as he expresses it, felt a soul in every muscle of his body, and his mind was filled with the thought that he was now going to earn his bread by his own labour.

The two young fellows parted at Inverary, and Campbell went on by way of Oban to Mull, reaching his destination after losing himself several times on the island, the entire length of which he says he traversed. His engagement was with a distant relative of his own, a Mrs Campbell, a 'worthy, sensible widow lady,' who treated him with thoughtful sympathy and consideration. What kind of tutor he made does not appear, but he evidently had the best intentions and a humane regard for his pupils. 'I never beat them,' he remarks, 'remembering how much I loved my father for having never beaten me.'

We know very little about this part of Campbell's career beyond what is told in his own letters. He expected to find in Mull 'a calm retreat for study and the Muses,' and he was not disappointed. At first, naturally enough, he felt very dejected. The house of Sunipol, where he taught, is on the northern shore of the island, from which a magnificent prospect of thirteen of the Hebrides group, including Staffa and Iona, can be obtained. The scenery, on Campbell's own admission, is 'marked by sublimity and the wild majesty of nature,' but unhappily in bad weather—and there is not much good weather in Mull—the island is 'only fit for the haunts of the damned.' There was plenty to feed the fancy of a poet; and yet, 'God wot,' says Campbell, 'I was better pleased to look on the kirk steeples and whinstone causeways of Glasgow than on all the eagles and wild deer of the Highlands.' His trunk was some days late in arriving, and as there was no writing paper in the island he was driven to the expedient of scribbling his thoughts on the wall of his room! However, he soon got reconciled to his forlorn condition; nay, in time he 'blessed the wild delight of solitude.' He diverted himself by botanising, by shooting wild geese, and, poet like, by rowing about in the moonlight; and we hear of an excursion to Staffa and Iona which filled him with hitherto unexperienced emotions of pleasure.

There is even a whisper of a little love affair. A certain Caroline Fraser, a daughter of the minister of Inverary, came to visit at Sunipol. She was, according to Beattie, who knew her, a girl of 'radiant beauty,' and Campbell, being himself well-favoured in the matter of looks—he is described at this time as 'a fair and beautiful boy, with pleasant and winning manners and a mild and cheerful disposition'—it was only natural that the pair should draw together. It was to this lady that the poem in two parts, bearing her Christian name, was addressed. The first part, beginning 'I'll bid the hyacinth to blow,' was written in Mull; the second, 'Gem of the crimson-coloured even,' in the following year, when the young tutor was frequently able to avail himself of the hospitality of the 'adorable Miss Caroline's' family. Verses were also addressed to 'A Rural Beauty in Mull,' but there is nothing to show that the 'young Maria' thus celebrated was anything more than a poetic creation. Of what may be called serious work during the course of the Mull tutorship we do not hear much. An Elegy, written in low spirits soon after he landed, was highly praised by Dr Anderson, the editor of the 'British Poets,' who predicted from it that the author would become a great poet; but Campbell showed himself a better critic when he characterised it as 'very humdrum indeed.' Many of his leisure hours were filled up with translations of his favourite classics, notably with what he calls his old comedy of the 'Clouds' of Aristophanes, but of these it is unnecessary to speak. The real effect of the Mull residence upon his poetic product was not felt until later. It might be too much to say that 'Lord Ullin's Daughter,' 'Lochiel,' and 'Glenara' would never have been written but for the author's sojourn in the Highlands, but the imagery of these and other pieces is clearly traceable to the promptings of island solitude; and much as Campbell disliked his isolation at the time, it undoubtedly proved of the greatest poetic service to him. Meanwhile, after five months of the wilderness, the exile became irksome, and he returned to Glasgow, glad to behold the kirk steeples and to feel his feet not on the 'bent' of Mull, but on the pavement of his native city.

Campbell now entered on his last session at the University. There is no detailed account of his studies this session, but he remarks himself, in his high-flown style, that the winter was one in which his mind advanced to a more expansive desire of knowledge than he had ever before experienced. He mentions especially the lectures of Professor Millar on Heineccius and on Roman Law. 'To say that Millar gave me *liberal* opinions would be understating the obligation which I either owed, or imagined I owed to him. He did more. He made investigations into the principles of justice and the rights and interests of society so captivating to me that I formed opinions for myself and became an emancipated lover of truth.' The impulse which Millar's lectures gave to his mind continued long after he heard them. At the time, they seem to have turned his thoughts very seriously towards the law as a profession. 'Poetry itself, in my love of jurisprudence and history,' he says, 'was almost forgotten. At that period, had I possessed but a few hundred pounds to have subsisted upon studying law, I believe I should have bid adieu to the Muses and gone to the Bar; but I had no choice in the matter.' As it was, the Muses during this session, and for some time after, appear to have received but scant attention. For a whole year he wrote nothing but the lines on Miss Broderick which still retain a place among his published works, and the two poems which gained him his parting prizes at the University. The latter were, it is assumed, sketched out in Mull. One was a translation from the 'Choephoroe,' the other of a Chorus in the 'Medea' of Euripides, the only prize piece which he afterwards included among his printed poems.

During the whole of this last session at the University he supported himself by private tuition. Among other pupils he had the future Lord Cunninghame of the Court of Session, who indeed boarded with the Campbell family in order to have the benefit of reading Greek with the son. Cunninghame says that Campbell left on his mind a deep impression, not merely of his abilities as a classical scholar, but of the elevation and purity of his sentiments. He read much in Demosthenes and Cicero, and enlarged on their eloquence and the grandeur of their views. It was by these ancient models that he tested the oratory of the moderns. He would repeat with the greatest enthusiasm the most impassioned passages of Lord Chatham's speeches on behalf of American freedom, and Burke's declamation against Warren Hastings was often on his lips. He was firmly convinced at this time that the rulers of the universe were in league against mankind, but he looked forward with some hope to the joyful day when the wrongs of society would be vindicated, and freedom again assume the ascendant. Lord Cunninghame draws a charming picture of the fireside politicians, with Campbell at their head, discussing the French Revolution, and defending their ultra-liberal opinions against the assaults of outsiders. For his age the poet probably took the world and the powers that be much too seriously; but his early political leanings are not without a certain significance in view of his after interest in the cause of liberty.

His last session at the University ended, Campbell, in June 1796, returned to Argyllshire, again as a tutor. This time his engagement was at Downie, near Lochgilphead. The house stood in a secluded spot on the shore of that great arm of the sea known as the Sound of Jura. The view to be obtained from its neighbourhood made a wonderful combination of sea and mountain scenery; but, like Sunipol, the place was altogether too dull for the city-bred youth. Campbell speaks of himself as living the life of a poor starling, caged in by rocks and seas from the haunts of man; as 'lying dormant in a solitary nook of the world, where there is nothing to chase the spleen,' and where the people 'seem to moulder away in sluggishness and deplorable ignorance.' Still, it was not quite so bad as Mull. For one thing, Inverary was comparatively near, and Hamilton Paul was there, as well as the adorable Caroline, to whose charms Paul, as appears from a poetical tribute, had also succumbed. Campbell, we may be sure, was oftener at Inverary than his letters show, for the 'Hebe of the West' clearly had magnetic powers of a quite unusual kind.

Paul has a lively account of the last day he spent with his friend at Inverary. It was the occasion of a 'frugal dinner,' when two old college companions joined the tutors around the table at the Inverary Arms. 'Never,' says Paul, 'did schoolboy enjoy an unexpected holiday more than Campbell. He danced, sang, and capered, half frantic with joy. Had he been only invested with the philabeg, he would have exhibited a striking resemblance to little Donald, leaping and dancing at a Highland wedding.' The company had a delightful afternoon together, and on the way home Campbell worked himself up into a state of ecstacy. He 'recited poetry of his own composition—some of which has never been printed—and then, after a moment's pause, addressed me: "Paul, you and I must go in search of adventures. If you will personate Roderick Random, I will go through the world with you as Strap." "Yes, Tom," said I, "I perceive what is to be the result: you are to be a poet by profession."'

Campbell's greatest difficulty at present was to settle upon any profession; but if his penchant for reciting poetry in the open air could have made him a poet, then indeed was his title clear. He told Scott some years after this that he repeated the 'Cadzow Castle' verses so often, stamping and shaking his head ferociously, while walking along the North Bridge of Edinburgh, that all the coachmen knew him by tongue, and quizzed him as he passed. The habit was mad enough in Edinburgh; in the Highlands it evidently suggested something like lunacy. His successor in the tutorship says that in Campbell's frequent walks along the shore he was often observed by the natives to be 'in a state of high and rapturous excitement,' of the cause and tendency of which they formed very strange and inconsistent ideas.

If the simple natives had suspected that the tutor was in love, they might, without knowing their Shakespeare, have paid less heed to these manifestations. Campbell had told Paul some time before that a poet should have only his muse for mistress; but it was easier to preach the precept than to practise it. It is in a letter to his friend Thomson that we first hear of this amourette. Speaking of a temporary brightening of his prospects, he says: 'To console me still further (but Thomson, I challenge your secrecy by all our former friendship), my evening walks are sometimes accompanied by *one* who, for a twelvemonth past, has won my purest but most ardent affection.

"Dear, precious name! rest ever unreveal'd,

Nor pass these lips in holy silence seal'd."

You may well imagine how the consoling words of such a person warm my heart into ecstacy of a most delightful kind. I say no more at present; and, my friend, I rely on your secrecy.' Campbell's secret has been kept, for the identity of this particular Amanda has never been disclosed. Can it have been the adorable Caroline herself? Whoever she was, she had, if we may trust Beattie, a very favourable influence in promoting Campbell's appeals to the muse. Defeated in all other prospects, he took refuge in 'the enchanted garden of love,' and, in the interchange of mutual affection, found compensation for all his disappointments.

But Campbell had his duties as a tutor to attend to. His pupil was the future Sir William Napier of Milliken, a great-great-grandson of the celebrated Napier of Merchiston. He was now about eight years old, and was living with his mother at Downie, his grandfather's estate. His father, Colonel Napier, returned from the West Indies shortly after Campbell entered on his engagement. Campbell describes him as 'a most agreeable gentleman, with all the mildness of a scholar and the majesty of a British Grenadier.' The Colonel took an eager interest in the tutor's welfare, and did all he could to settle him in some permanent employment. 'He has,' says Campbell to Thomson, 'been active to consult, to advise, to recommend me, with warmth and success, and that to friends of the first rank.' With a local physician he united to obtain for him a favourable situation in the office of a leading Edinburgh lawyer, but unfortunately a combination of circumstances baffled the poet's aims in this direction; and, the term of his engagement having expired, he returned once more to Glasgow, in a state of the greatest concern about his future. 'I will,' he declared, with that unnecessary rhetoric to which he was prone, 'I will maintain my independence by lessening my wants, if I should live upon a barren heath.'

CHAPTER III
'THE PLEASURES OF HOPE'

Campbell was now at his wit's end about a profession. With whatever intention he had gone to the University, he had at last become alive to the stern fact that the University had done nothing for him in regard to a livelihood. 'What,' he wanted to know, 'have all these academical honours procured for me?' He was dissatisfied with himself for his admitted lack of resource; he was dissatisfied with his friends for their apathetic indifference. But something had clearly to be done, and after sundry ineffectual efforts to reach a solid standing ground, he again turned his attention to the law. 'That is the line which he means to pursue,' wrote his sister Elizabeth, 'and what I think nature has just fitted him for. He is a fine public speaker and I have no doubt will make a figure at the Bar.' His idea now was to combine law with literature. Let him once get into a lawyer's office and he would have no fear of working his way without the expense of entrance fees. He would write for the leading periodicals and establish a magazine. He had, besides, one or two translations from the classics nearly ready for the press, and for these surely some publisher, he told himself, would be willing to pay.

In this optimistic mood he went off to Edinburgh, the home of literature and law, where he arrived in May, 1797. His old pupil, Lord Cunninghame, was now preparing for the Bar, and to him Campbell applied for aid in finding employment. The employment was found, not in a law office—for Campbell had no regular training as a law clerk to recommend him—but in the Register House, where the University honours' man was set to the humble tasks of a copying clerk. A few weeks of extract making proved enough for him, and he threw up the situation for one slightly more comfortable, though not much better as to pay, in the office of a Mr Bain Whytt. There he remained, sucking sustenance through a quill, until Dr Anderson brought him forth to put him on the road to renown.

Campbell was introduced to Anderson by Mr Hugh Park, then a teacher in Glasgow, who had roused an interest in the poetical clerk by showing a copy of the elegy written in Mull. Miss Anderson was present at the first meeting, and Beattie subsequently obtained from her some recollections of the occasion. She remarked specially upon Campbell's good looks. His face, she said, was beautiful, and 'the pensive air which hung so gracefully over his youthful features gave a melancholy interest to his manner which was extremely touching.' This description, it may be observed, is in part corroborated from other quarters. The Rev. Dr Wardlaw, who had been one of Campbell's classfellows at Glasgow, said that though he was comparatively small in stature his features were handsome and prepossessing, and were characterised by an intelligent animation and a cheerful openness all the more noticeable that they gave place when he was not pleased to 'a gravity approaching to sternness.' Another friend speaks of him as an ardent, enthusiastic boy, much younger in appearance than in years. Unfortunately there is no portrait of him at this early age.

Dr Anderson took a fervent interest in the pensive youth. He knew everybody worth knowing, and through him Campbell soon found his way into the best literary society of the capital. Scott, Jeffrey, Dugald Stewart, Lord Brougham, Henry Mackenzie, the 'Man of Feeling,' George Thomson, the correspondent of Burns—these and others, in addition to the friends he had made on former visits, were now or later among the circle of his acquaintances. At a private house he met that 'pompous ass,' the Earl of Buchan, and apparently had the bad manners to quiz him upon his oddities. It was at this time, too, that he was introduced to John Leyden, with whom he afterwards so notoriously fell out. There are two explanations of the quarrel. According to the first, Leyden had spread a report that, in despair at his prospects, Campbell was seen one day rushing frantically along Princes Street on the way to destroy himself. This foolish story was revived after Campbell's death; very likely it was quite unfounded. The other version of the affair is to the effect that Campbell, by his association with certain infidel youths who had started a publication called the *Clerical Review*, allowed it to be inferred that some of his intimate friends, including Anderson and Leyden, were in sympathy with the unsettling tendencies of the new journal. There was no reason why anybody should draw such an inference; and, in any case, the explanation is unsatisfactory inasmuch as the quarrel was evidently of Campbell's, not of Leyden's making. Whatever be the solution— and it is not a matter of importance—there was certainly no love lost between Leyden and his somewhat prim junior. Campbell seldom mentions Leyden's name without a sneer. In a letter of 1803 he says: 'London has been visited in one month by John Leyden and the influenza. They are both raging with great violence.' And again—the versatile Borderer had just taken a surgeon's diploma—'Leyden has gone at last to diminish the population of India.' Nevertheless, as we shall learn later on, Campbell knew very well how to value the critical opinion of John Leyden—when it was in his favour.

But Dr Anderson did more for Campbell than present him to his literary circle. Campbell, though he proclaimed his dislike of another tutorship, had expressed his willingness to accept almost any kind of literary work. Anderson accordingly introduced him to Mundell, the publisher, and the result was an offer of twenty guineas for an abridged edition of Bryan Edwards' 'West Indies.' This was not only Campbell's first undertaking for the press, but the first of his many pieces of literary task-work. He was now anticipating very much the later experience of Carlyle, who also tried the law in Edinburgh, and became a bookseller's hack when that 'bog-pool of disgust' proved impossible. But there the parallel ends.

Campbell went back to Glasgow, walking the distance as usual, to finish his abridgment. His mind was still exercised about the future. Anything in the law beyond the most laborious plodding he had seen to be quite out of his reach. 'I have fairly tried the business of an attorney,' he wrote, 'and upon my conscience it is the most accursed of all professions. Such meanness, such toil, such contemptible modes of peculation were never moulded into one profession... It is true there are many emoluments; but I declare to God that I can hardly spend with a safe conscience the little sum I made during my residence in Edinburgh.' This, of course, is not to be taken seriously: it is merely the petulant cry of a spoilt and conceited youth. Campbell confessed afterwards that at this time fame was everything to him. So far as at present appeared he was as likely to achieve fame as to extract sunbeams from cucumbers, and when he miscalled the lawyers as rogues and vagabonds he was only giving voice to his chagrin.

But youth is not easily dismayed. It was at this moment that, having saved a little money, Campbell gaily proposed to start a magazine. He invited some of his college familiars to join with him, declaring that he would undertake, if need be, three-fourths of the letter-press himself. 'We shall,' he remarked, 'set all the magazine scribblers at defiance—nay, hold them even in profound contempt.' But his friends were not so sanguine about sharing the favours of a 'discerning public,' and the magazine project, like so many other projects, fell to the ground. It shows the desperate frame of mind into which Campbell had sunk, that, in spite of his recent 'malediction upon the law and all its branches,' he still professed himself an amateur of the Bar. He tells Anderson that his leisure hours are employed on Godwin and the 'Corpus Juris.' The latter he had always regarded as a somniferous volume, but now he finds that there is something really amusing as well as improving in the book. It certainly does not seem a suitable work for stimulating the imagination of a poet, but Campbell was only playing with circumstances after all. Even yet he may have had some idea that the 'Corpus Juris' would prove professionally useful.

In the meantime he went on with his abridgment, and wrote a few verses. Among the latter was 'The Wounded Hussar,' a lyric suggested by an incident in one of the recent battles on the Danube. This ballad, now entirely forgotten, attained an extraordinary popularity. It had been published only a few weeks when all Glasgow was ringing with it. Subsequently it found its way to London, where it was sung on the streets and encored in the theatres. It seemed as if the fame for which the author hungered was to be his at last, but curiously enough, in this case he would have none of it. 'That accursed song,' he would say, and forbid his friends to mention 'The Wounded

Hussar' again in his presence. About this time also he wrote his 'Lines on revisiting Cathcart,' besides a 'Dirge of Wallace,' which he sensibly excluded from his collected works as being too rhapsodical, though it was often printed against his wish in the Galignani editions.

Having finished his work for Mundell, Campbell returned to Edinburgh in the autumn of 1797. What his plans now were is not very clear, though from the fact that he spoke to his parents about following him when his circumstances permitted, it is evident that he had made up his mind to reside permanently in the capital. At present his prospects were as gloomy as ever. Mundell had promised him some employment for the winter, and a further slight engagement on a contemplated geographical work seemed probable. At the best, however, these were but feeble supports; the booksellers—who, he enquired, could depend on *them*? Some time before this he had, as we have seen, tried medicine and surgery and failed; now, as a sort of forlorn hope, he again betook himself to the study of chemistry and anatomy. That, too, was soon abandoned, and he fell back once more on the *dernier resort* of a tutorship. By and by his younger brother Robert sent him a pressing invitation to come out to Virginia, and he decided to quit Scotland in the spring of 1798. But here again his design was defeated; his elder brother in Demerara wisely interposed his experienced advice against it, and Campbell's oft-expressed desire to see the land of Washington was never realised.

In all these shifting plans and projects one discerns thus early what proved the chief defect in Campbell's character—that irresolution and that caprice which were so largely to blame for many of the vexations and disappointments of his later life. No doubt to some extent his friends were responsible for his unsteadiness of purpose. He was the Benjamin of his family, petted and pampered, applauded for his little clevernesses, and encouraged in his belief that he had been cut out for something great. Had he been alone in the world, and absolutely penniless, he would have had to exert himself to some purpose. As it was, he never stuck at an honest calling long enough to know what he could do at it; but having tried many things perfunctorily, and failed in them, he at length derived inspiration from his empty pocket, braced himself to what after all was most congenial to him, and in a sense, like Silas Wegg, 'dropped into poetry.'

Speaking afterwards of this period, he says: 'I lived in the Scottish metropolis by instructing pupils in Greek and Latin. In that vocation I made a comfortable livelihood as long as I was industrious. But "The Pleasures of Hope" came over me. I took long walks about Arthur's Seat, conning over my own (as I thought) magnificent lines; and as my "Pleasures of Hope" got on, my pupils fell off.' Here we have the first intimation that Campbell was actually working upon the poem by which he made his grand entry on the stage of public life. But the subject had engaged his thoughts long before this. So far back as 1795, when slaving as a tutor in Mull, he had asked his friend Hamilton Paul to send him 'some lines consolatory to a hermit.' Paul replied with a set of verses on 'The Pleasures of Solitude,' adding: 'We have now three "Pleasures" by first-rate men of genius—"The Pleasures of Imagination," "The Pleasures of Memory," and "The Pleasures of Solitude." Let us cherish "The Pleasures of Hope" that we may soon meet in *Alma Mater.*'

The subject thus playfully suggested dwelt in Campbell's mind; and although there is nothing to show that he at once began the composition of the poem, there is every reason to believe that some parts of it had been at least drafted during his two periods of exile in the Highlands. At any rate, in his 'dusky lodging' in Rose Street he now set to work upon it in earnest; and by the close of 1798 it was being shown to his private circle as practically ready for the press. Campbell's intention appears to have been to publish it by subscription, and on that understanding a friend gave him £15 to pay for the printing. Dr Anderson, however, intervened; and after he had discussed the merits of the poem with Mundell, the latter bought the entire copyright, as the note of agreement has it, 'for two hundred copies of the book in quires.' This would mean something over £50, the volume having been published at six shillings. At the time Campbell probably thought the bargain fair enough, but he naturally took a different view of the case after some thousands of copies of the poem had been sold. It was, he said towards the end of his life, worth an annuity of £200, but he added that he must not forget how for two or three years the publishers gave him £50 for every new edition. When we recall the fact that for 'Paradise Lost' Milton got exactly £10, we must regard Campbell as having been unusually well paid.

After being subjected to a great deal of correction, mainly at the instigation of Anderson, to whom it was dedicated, 'The Pleasures of Hope' was published on the 29th of April, 1799, when the poet was twenty-one years and nine months old. It had been announced as in the press some time before, and there was now a brisk demand for copies, four editions being called for in the first year. So early a success had only a near parallel in the case of Byron, who awoke to find himself famous at twenty-four. The author, it was remarked, had suddenly emerged like a star from his obscurity, and had thrown a brilliant light over the literary horizon of his country. His poem was quoted as 'an epitome of sound morals, inculcating by lofty examples the practice of every domestic virtue, and conveying the most instructive lessons in the most harmonious language.' One critic said it gave fair promise of his rivalling some of the greatest poets of modern times; another critic commended it for its sublimity of conception, its boldness of imagery, its vigour of language and its manliness of sentiment. And so they swelled the chorus, to the same tune of extravagant eulogy.

Much of the success of the poem was no doubt due to the circumstance that it touched with such sympathy on the burning questions of the hour. If, as Stevenson remarks, the poet is to speak efficaciously, he must say what is already in his hearer's mind. This Campbell did, as perhaps no English poet had done before. The French Revolution, the partition of Poland, the abolition of negro-slavery—these had set the passion for freedom burning in many breasts, and 'The Pleasures of Hope' gave at once vigorous and feeling expression to the doctrine of the universal brotherhood of man. Moreover, the moment was favourable in that there were so few rivals in the field. Burns had been dead for three years, and Rogers might now be said to stand alone in the front rank. Crabbe, suffering under domestic sorrow, had been all but silent since his 'Village' appeared in 1783; Cowper was sunk in hopeless insanity. Neither Wordsworth nor Coleridge, both older than Campbell, had secured a following; Scott had printed but a few translations from the German. Byron was at school, Moore at college; Hogg had not spoken, and Southey's fame was still to make. There could hardly have been a stronger case of the *felix opportunitate*.

It is not easy at this time of day to approach 'The Pleasures of Hope' without a want of sympathy, if not an absolute prejudice, resulting from a whole century of poetical development. The ideals, the standards of Campbell's day, have wholly altered; were indeed passing away even in his own time. The little volume of 'Lyrical Ballads,' published only a few months before Campbell's poem, sounded, as it has been expressed, the clarion-call of the new poetry. The manner thus introduced by Wordsworth and Coleridge completely changed the critical standpoint; and it is perfectly safe to say that any poem which appeared to-day with the opening line of 'The Pleasures of Hope'—'At summer eve, when heaven's *ethereal bow*'—would meet with very severe treatment at the hands of the critics, if indeed the critics condescended to notice it at all.

Further, too much stress must not be laid on the fact, already referred to, and always so carefully stated by the school editors, that the poem met with a phenomenal success on its first appearance. In literature popularity bears no strict proportion to merit. Neither Keats nor Shelley nor Wordsworth was ever 'popular'; of 'The Christian,' we are given to understand, a hundred copies were sold for every one of 'Richard Feverel.' The popularity of 'The Pleasures of Hope' might easily have been foretold by any one reading it before publication, not for any poetic excellence it possessed—though it was not without poetic excellence—but because it accorded so well with the prevalent moods and opinions of a large section of the public at the time. Given certain vulgar ideas, the power of fluent and forcible expression, and no great depth of thought or subtlety of imagination, and the breath of popular applause may generally be counted upon.

In poets youth, when not a virtue, is at least an extenuating circumstance. Campbell was very young when he wrote 'The Pleasures of Hope.' At an age when an Englishman is midway in his University course, and perhaps thinking of competing for the Newdigate, Campbell had finished his college career, won all the possible honours, and got himself accepted at his own valuation as 'demnition clever.' He was only a boy, a clever boy, with boyish enthusiasms, boyish crudities of thought, and, it must be confessed, a boyish weakness for fine-sounding words. His poem was not the spontaneous fruit of his imagination. There was no inward compulsion to poetic utterance as in the case of other poets who wrote at an equally early age. The clever boy was moping, without definite aims, when his friend's suggestion conjured up a vision of Thomas Campbell admitted to the company of Mark Akenside and Samuel Rogers. True, these names were not the brightest in the poetical galaxy, and it might perhaps have been better for Campbell if he had schooled himself by a diligent study of Milton and Spenser. But there was the goal, and there was the motive, and he set about his poem.

Undoubtedly he made the most of what could easily have proved a barren theme. The construction of the poem is certainly loose; part does not follow part in any inevitable order. But in a didactic poem this is perhaps an advantage, for, with all its defects, one can read 'The Pleasures of Hope' without the fatigue that accompanies a reading of 'The Pleasures of Imagination.' To analyse the poem would be superfluous. It faithfully reflected the common thought of the time, and assuredly does not, as Beattie said it did, give illumination to 'every succeeding age.' It will be sufficient to point out a few of its literary qualities with a view to an appreciation of Campbell's place as a poet.

And first it must be remarked that Campbell was subdued to the vicious theory of a poetical diction. To him a rainbow was an 'ethereal bow,' a musket a 'glittering tube,' a star a 'pensile orb,' a cottage a 'rustic dome.' It was a principle with him and his school that the ordinary name of a thing, the natural way of saying a thing, must necessarily be unpoetic. This comes out equally in his letters. When he refers to a railway train it is as 'a chariot of fire.' Instead of saying: 'I went to the club with his Lordship,' he must say: 'Thither with his Lordship I accordingly repaired.' When he wishes to speak of a thing being 'changed' into another, he says it is 'transported to the identity of' that other thing. In 'The Pleasures of Hope' this characteristic was no doubt due in some cases to the exigence of rhyme, which probably accounts also for the so-called obscurity of certain of his lines. For he is not really obscure; his stream is too shallow for obscurity. On that point it is curious to note how even Wordsworth was misled. Perhaps it may be worth while to quote what he says:

Campbell's 'Pleasures of Hope' has been strangely overrated. Its fine words and sounding lines please the generality of readers, who never stop to ask themselves the meaning of a passage. The lines—

> Where Andes, giant of the western star,
>
> With meteor standard to the wind unfurled,
>
> Looks from his throne of clouds o'er half the world,

are sheer nonsense—nothing more than a poetical indigestion. What has a giant to do with a star? What is a meteor standard? But it is useless to inquire what such stuff means. Once at my house Professor Wilson, having spoken of these lines with great admiration, a very sensible and accomplished lady, who happened to be present, begged him to explain to her their meaning. He was extremely indignant, and taking down 'The Pleasures of Hope' from a shelf, read the lines aloud, and declared they were splendid. 'Well, sir,' said the lady, 'but *what do they mean?*' Dashing down the book on the floor, he exclaimed in his broad Scotch accent, 'I'll be daumed if I can tell.'

The explanation is, however, simple enough. Campbell obviously meant 'firmament' or 'hemisphere,' but wanting a rhyme to 'afar,' he put the part for the whole, and said 'western star.' This is not exactly obscurity; but for the fact that Campbell was always so careful to polish his verse we should call it clumsiness.

In his management of the heroic couplet, Campbell was eminently successful. With the monosyllabic rhyme the lines naturally end rather monotonously with a snap as it were: *enjambement* is not frequent; the verse has nothing of that freedom and fluidity in which Chaucer and Keats are sworn brothers. But Campbell varies the position of the pause more frequently than Pope, and he actually excels Pope in respect of rhyme; for, with all his correctness, Pope was an indifferent rhymster. Apart from his imperfect rhymes, which are sufficiently numerous, one finds in Pope whole blocks of six or eight lines ending in intolerable assonances. Campbell is never guilty of this fault; and even in the smaller sin of harping over much on the same rhyme, he is no worse than Pope. Further, he is very deft in 'suiting the sound to the sense.' Many lines might be quoted which are full of such music as springs from a varied succession of vowel sounds linked by alliterative consonants. In bringing sounding names into his verse, too, he is as expert as Goldsmith himself. Oonalaska, Seriswattee, Kosciusko—these are names to conjure with. And if 'rapture' does duty too often for ardent emotion of all kinds, if 'tumultuous' comes too trippingly off the pen when an epithet is required—well, let us remember again that he was very young. The poem was at least a credit to his years. Vigour, variety, pleasant description, sincere rhetoric, youthful fervour and high spirits account in the main for its popularity. Its concrete illustrations, its little *genre* scenes, saved it from the fate of most didactic poems on abstract themes. The homely interior, the returned wanderer, the cradle, the faithful dog—these appealed to the average man; and the political allusions struck the right note for the times. But who reads it now?

Before the publication of 'The Pleasures of Hope' Campbell was practically a nonentity; after that event he became a literary lion. His experience was that of Burns over again on a smaller scale; indeed some of the distinguished men who had hailed Burns' arrival in the capital were still alive to give their acclamations to Campbell, whom they may not unlikely have regarded as a possible successor. Scott invited him to dinner and proposed his health amid a strong muster of his literary friends. Dr Gregory—whose name has survived in connection with what Stevenson calls 'our good old Scotch medicine'—discovered his poem on Mundell's counter fresh from the printer, and at once sought him out. Everybody wanted to meet him; and invitations poured in upon him until, like Sterne after the publication of 'Tristram Shandy,' he found himself deep in social engagements for months ahead. How he bore it all we have no means of knowing. Thirty years later he speaks of himself as being at this time 'a young, shrinking, bashful creature,' though he is honest enough to add that he had a very high opinion of himself and his powers. Probably the right measure of his timidity was taken by the lady who described him as 'swaggering about' in a Suwarrow jacket.

With the exception of 'Gilderoy,' Campbell does not seem to have written anything during the remainder of 1799. He conceived the idea of a poem on 'the patriot Tell,' but notwithstanding that the subject must have been exactly to his liking he never utilised it. Another idea which occurred to him also failed of fruition, although references continue to be made to it in his correspondence for some time. This was a poem to be called 'The Queen of the North,' in which—with Edinburgh as the *locale*—such themes as the independence of Scotland and the achievements of her great men were to be employed to revive the old spirit of freedom. In the meantime, while these projects were passing through his mind, a new edition of 'The Pleasures of Hope' had been called for, and with Mundell's additional payment of £50 in his pocket, Campbell decided to make a tour in Germany.

The objects to be gained by this pilgrimage were perfectly plain to him. He would acquire another language, and he would enlarge his views of society. In the conversation of his travelled friends he could detect the advantages of intercourse with the foreigner, and in travelling, as they had travelled, he hoped to rid himself of the imputation that 'home-keeping youths have ever homely wits.' In spite of his recent poetic performance, he felt that he was still a raw youth, who would make but a poor figure in a company of London wits; and although he expected to be stared at for his awkwardness and ridiculed for his broken German, yet, to be 'uncaged from the insipid scenes of life,' to 'see the wonders of the world abroad,' to make first-hand acquaintance with that literature, so prominently represented by Goethe, which was then rising like a star on the intellectual world—all this he regarded as a compensation for greater evils than his friends could suggest or his fears imagine.

For one must not forget that the contemplated tour was not without some risks. The year 1800 was not exactly the time that one who valued above all things his personal comfort, perhaps even his personal liberty, would have chosen for a continental holiday. The long wars of the French Revolution had been in progress for some time, and Napoleon had just begun to make himself famous. England was at war with France; France was at war with Austria, and Russia had formed a coalition with Sweden and Denmark against England. In short, Europe was at the time in such a state of military unrest that no one knew what a day or an hour might bring forth. But Campbell, living at home at ease, thought very lightly of the hazards of war. He was tired of his 'dully sluggardised' existence, without definite aim or ambition; and so, in the beginning of June, he walked down to Leith, and, with a sheaf of introductions in his pocket, set sail for Hamburg.

CHAPTER IV
CONTINENTAL TRAVELS

Campbell's intention had been to proceed from Harwich after a week's visit to London, but, on mature reflection, he decided that the 'modern Babel' must wait. Some months later he realised that he had made a mistake. 'It is a sad want not to be able to tell foreigners anything of London,' he then wrote; 'I have blushed for shame when the ladies asked me questions about it.' This, however, was a point he had not foreseen, and his immediate reasons for delaying the London visit were both frank and amusing. On the eve of his departure he explains to Thomson that he had resisted the seductions of the great city because his finances were not equal to both London and Germany, and Germany he would on no account forego. Moreover, he knew his own nature too well. New sights and new acquaintances would have dismissed the little industry he possessed, and would have soon reduced him to the fettered state of a bookseller's fag. There was still another consideration. He was not fitted for shining in a London company just yet. When he had added to the number of his books, he might think of making his *debût*, but for the present he would not run the risk of ridicule on account of his northern brogue and his 'braw Scotch boos.' And then comes this curious announcement: 'In reality my fixed intention on returning from Germany is to set up a course of lectures on the *Belles Lettres*. I had some thoughts of lecturing in Edinburgh, but cannot think of remaining any longer in one place. If London should not offer encouragement, I mean to try Dublin. I think this a respectable profession, as the showman of the bear and monkey said when he gave his name to the commissioners of the income tax as an "itinerant lecturer on natural history."' The last sentence suggests—though it is impossible to be sure, for Campbell's jokes were rather heavy-handed—that he threw out this idea in jest. If he was serious, it is another indication of his habit of easily adopting new professions, of which we may learn more in the sequel.

Campbell had a cordial reception from the British residents in Hamburg. He met Klopstock, and presented him with a copy of 'The Pleasures of Hope.' He describes the poet as 'a mild, civil old man,' one of the first really great men in the world of letters he ever knew, and adds that his only intercourse with him was in Latin, with which language he made his way tolerably well among the French and Germans, and still better among the Hungarians. How long he remained in Hamburg is not certain: as we shall see presently, he had arrived at Ratisbon in time to witness the startling military events of July. The political excitement was now at its height. Several of the Bavarian towns were in the hands of the French, and the upper valley of the Danube was under military government. 'Everything here,' says Campbell, writing soon after his arrival, 'is whisper, surmise, and suspense. If war breaks out, the bridge over the Danube is expected to be blown up. You may guess what a devil of a splutter twenty-four large arches will make flying miles high in the air and coming down like falling planets to crush the town!... Ratisbon will be shivered to atoms; and as no warning is expected, the inhabitants may be buried under the ruins.'

To be thus plunged, as it were, into the thick of the fray was hardly a pleasant experience for the British pilgrim. The richest fields of Europe desolated by contending troops; peasants driven from their homes to starve and beg in the streets; horses dying of hunger, and men dying of their wounds—such were the 'dreadful novelties' that Campbell had come from Edinburgh to see. He describes the whole thing very vividly in letters to his eldest brother. The following refers particularly to the action which gave the French possession of Ratisbon. He says:

I got down to the seat of war some weeks before the summer armistice, and indulged in what you call the criminal curiosity of witnessing blood and desolation. Never shall time efface from my memory the recollection of that hour of astonishment when I stood with the good monks of St James' to overlook a charge of Klenau's cavalry upon the French under Grenier. We saw the fire given and returned, and heard distinctly the sound of French *pas de charge* collecting the lines to attack in close column. After three hours awaiting the issue of a severe action, a park of artillery was opened just beneath the walls of the monastery, and several drivers that were stationed there to convey the wounded in spring waggons were killed in our sight.

In some notes relating to the same period he remarks that, in point of impressions, this formed the most important epoch in his life; but he adds that his recollections of seeing men strewn dead on the field, or what was worse, seeing them dying, were so horrible, that he studiously endeavoured to banish them from his memory.

There were, however, scenes of peace as well as of war. Some Hamburg friends had given him letters of introduction to the venerable Abbot Arbuthnot, of the Benedictine Scots College, under whose protection it was believed that he would have special opportunities for study and observation; and the hospitality of the monks now 'amused' him, as he puts it, into such tranquillity as was possible in that perilous time. The 'splendour and sublimity' of the Catholic Church service, notably the music, also affected him with all the attraction of novelty. But these things were at best only alleviations. Campbell had already begun to suffer from Johnson's demon of hypochondria, and when the novelty of his surroundings had worn off, he felt himself in the worst imaginable plight of the stranger in a strange land.

The following programme of his day's doings affords a hint of his wretchedness:

I rise at seven—thanks to the flies that forbid me to sleep—and after returning thanks to God for prolonging my miserable existence at Ratisbon, I put on a pair of boots and pantaloons, and study with open windows, and half-naked, till ten o'clock. I then chew a crust of bread, and eat a plum for breakfast. At 11 my *parlez-vous-Français* steps in with his formal periwig and still more formal bow. I chatter a jargon of Latin and French to him—for he has no English—and study again from 12 till 1: dine and read English or Greek till 2, and then take an afternoon walk. Under a burning sun I then expose my feeble carcase in a walk round the cursed walls, or traverse the wood where the Rothmantels or 'Red Cloaks' and Hussars amused us at cut-and-thrust before the city was taken. Sometimes I venture to the heights where the last kick-up was seen, when the poor Austrians were driven across the Danube. The Convent I seldom visit: we always get upon politics, and that is a cursed subject.

So indeed it seemed. It was, however, Campbell's own fault. The brotherhood of the Schotten Kirche[2] had welcomed him very heartily on his arrival; but they were Jacobites, and he was so indiscreet as to make open avowal of his Republican opinions. The result was unpleasant enough. One of the monks denounced him for his political heresies; others regarded him with ill-concealed suspicion and distrust. A countryman of his own, who bore the conventual name of Father Boniface, had recommended him to an unsuitable lodging at the house of a friend, and Campbell complained that he had been robbed there. Father Boniface met the complaint with abuse, and 'spoke to me once or twice,' says Campbell, 'in a manner rather strange.' One night the Father dogged him into the refectory and attacked him with the most blackguardly scurrility. 'I never,' writes Campbell, 'found myself so completely carried away by indignation. I flew at the scoundrel and would have soon rewarded his insolence had not the others interposed.' After an experience like this, it was only natural that he should declaim against the 'lazy, loathsome, ignorant, ill-bred' monks, whose society he had at first found so agreeable! The only one for whom he entertained a lasting regard was Dr Arbuthnot, whom he describes as 'the most commanding figure he ever beheld,' and to whom he unmistakably alludes in 'The Ritter Bann,' one of his later poems.

Being unable either to advance or retreat, and not knowing what to do with himself amid the gloom and excitement caused by the presence of two hostile armies, Campbell appears to have sunk into something like blank despair. 'Oh, God!' he exclaims in a letter, 'when the dull dusk of evening comes on, when the melancholy bell calls to vespers, I find myself a poor solitary being, dumb from the want of heart to speak, and deaf to all that is said from a want of interest to hear.' About the future he feels an insecurity and a dread which baffle all his efforts to form a scheme or resolution. Low-minded people suspect him, and debate about his character, and wonder what he can be doing in Ratisbon. He cannot settle himself to literary work of any kind. He sits down resolved to compose in spite of uncertainty and uneasiness, and looks helplessly for hours together at the paper before him.

Campbell's letters of this period make indeed most doleful reading. They are addressed, for the most part, to John Richardson, a young Edinburgh lawyer who enjoyed familiar intercourse with Scott and other *dii majores* of the capital. Richardson had promised to join him in Germany, and when Campbell is not voicing his woes, he is planning schemes for Richardson and himself when at length they are free to start on a tour. With economy he thinks they might visit every corner of Germany, travel three thousand miles, stop at convenient stages for a few days at a time, and be 'masters of all the geographical knowledge worth learning' for £30 a-piece. They will require nothing in the way of baggage but 'a stick fitted as an umbrella—a nice contrivance very common here—with a fine Holland shirt in one pocket, our stockings and silk breeches in the other, and a few cravats wrapped in clean paper in the crowns of our hats.' At country inns they can have bed and supper for half-a-crown, coffee for sixpence, and bread and beer for twopence. As for books, Campbell will always manage to carry enough in his pockets for evening amusement; but Richardson must 'bring, for God's sake, Shakespeare and a few British classics.' A striking idea occurs to him in one of his sportive moods. 'Without degrading our characters in the least, we might have some articles from Britain and dispose of them to immense advantage. The merchants here are greedy and blind to their interests: they sell little because they sell so high. Their general profit is two hundred per cent.' The spectacle of Thomas Campbell hawking British goods round the German Empire would have been sufficiently diverting; but of course it was only another of his ponderous pleasantries.

Nevertheless, there was good reason for his being anxious about making a little money. His funds were fast giving out, and at present he did not quite see how he was to replenish his purse. He makes constant complaint about the uncertainty of remittances, and in one letter strikes his hand on his 'sad heart' as he thinks of himself starving far from home and friends. However, matters mended a little for a time: his spirits revived, he found himself able to work again; and the armistice having been renewed, he made various interesting excursions into the interior, getting as far as Munich, and returning by the valley of the Iser. 'I remember,' he says, speaking of these excursions in a letter quoted by Washington Irving, 'I remember how little I valued the art of painting before I got into the heart of such impressive scenes; but in Germany I would have given anything to have possessed an art capable of conveying ideas inaccessible to speech and writing. Some particular scenes were indeed rather overcharged with that degree of the terrific which oversteps the sublime; and I own my flesh yet creeps at the recollection of spring-waggons and hospitals. But the sight of Ingolstadt in ruins or Hohenlinden covered with fire, seven miles in circumference, were spectacles never to be forgotten.'

The reference to Hohenlinden here is somewhat puzzling. According to Beattie, Campbell left Ratisbon in the beginning of October, and went by way of Leipsic to Altona, where he remained until his return to England. He was certainly at Altona in the beginning of November, for his letters then begin to date from thence. But the battle of Hohenlinden was not fought until the 3rd of December, and it is therefore clear that Campbell, unless he made a journey of which we have no trace, could not have seen Hohenlinden 'covered with fire.' Beattie suggests that in the passage just quoted Hohenlinden may be a slip for Landshut on the Iser, Leipheim, near Gunzberg, or Donauwert, where battles and conflagrations took place during the summer campaign, the effects of which Campbell may have witnessed after his arrival on the Danube. He says that he often heard the poet refer to 'the sight of Ingolstadt in ruins,' but he never once heard him describe the field of Hohenlinden. Of course if he visited Munich at the time mentioned he may have made a cursory survey of the village; but until after the battle, travellers never thought of going out of their way to see Hohenlinden. It is a pity that there should be any dubiety upon this matter, for our interest in Campbell's stirring lines would have been heightened by the knowledge that he had been an eye-witness of the events which they describe.

The armistice which had been renewed at Hohenlinden on the 28th of September was for forty-five days. As the time for its termination approached Campbell thought it wise, in view of a resumption of hostilities, to secure his passports, and escape from Ratisbon. There was another determining point: his funds were now almost exhausted, and he wanted to be nearer home. He decided to go to Hamburg, whence, if remittances did not arrive, he could take passage for Leith. Of his journey from Ratisbon we hear practically nothing, though in one of his letters he gives an indication of his route by mentioning such towns as Nuremberg, Bamberg, Weimar, Jena, Leipsic, Halle, Brunswick, and Lunenburg. In his previous journey to Ratisbon in July he seems to have followed the course of the Elbe to Dresden, and thence proceeded through Zwickau, Bayreuth, and Amberg to the seat of war on the Danube; so that now he was, as he says, 'master of all to be seen' in a very considerable part of the country.

When he reached Hamburg he found a letter awaiting him from Richardson announcing that a 'blessed double edition' of 'The Pleasures of Hope' had been thrown off, thus entitling him to £50, according to the understanding with Mundell. Relieved of all his pecuniary anxiety in this unexpected fashion, Campbell resolved to remain abroad for the winter. He took up his quarters at Altona, a town near Hamburg, which he describes as the pleasantest place in all Germany. His letters begin to show a more cheerful spirit. He has the prospect of 'useful and agreeable acquaintance, and a winter of useful activity,' and his portfolio, hitherto a chaos, is soon to be filled with 'monsters and wonders sufficient to match the pages of Bruce himself.' One of the new acquaintances promised to prove of substantial advantage to him. A gentleman of family preparing for a tour along the lower Danube, required a travelling companion, and having been introduced to Campbell, he offered him £100 a year to accompany him and direct his studies. There was to be nothing like a formal tutorship; the poet was merely to make himself a 'respectable friend and useful companion.' Campbell professed to be at this time, like Burns, sorely touchable on the score of independence, but a man who has to content himself, as Campbell had now to do, with two meals a day, must find it convenient to swallow his pride occasionally; and Campbell, after a great deal of epistolary fuss about it, accepted the gentleman's offer.

Unfortunately the agreement was never carried out. Beattie's curt intimation is that 'sudden and important changes' took place in the views and circumstances of the anticipated patron. We get, however, an inkling of the real state of the case from a letter of Campbell's to Dr Anderson, written from London some months later—a letter which does equal honour to the poet's kind-heartedness and modesty. Speaking of his well-intentioned friend he says:

That valuable and high-spirited young man was humbled—after a struggle which concealed misfortunes—to reveal his situation and in sickness to receive assistance from one whose advancement and re-establishment in life he had planned but a few weeks before, when no reverse of fortune was dreaded. His situation required more than my resources were adequate to impart, but still it prevented his feelings being deeply wounded by addressing strangers. I did not regret my own share of the hardships, but I acknowledge that in those days of darkness and distress I had hardly spirit to write a single letter. I have often left the sick-bed of my friend for a room of my own which wanted the heat of a fire in the month of January, and on the borders of Denmark.

The failure of this enterprise was obviously a great disappointment to Campbell. The prospects of the tour had seemed to him peculiarly enticing, and he never ceased to deplore the necessity which led to its being abandoned.

Another acquaintance made at this time happily bore some fruit. A certain Anthony M'Cann, 'a brave United Irishman,' had, with other unfortunate fellow-countrymen who were engaged in the Rebellion of 1798, taken refuge on the banks of the Elbe. Campbell fell in with him and his fellow exiles, and passed a good part of his leisure in their society. The literary result was that pathetic if somewhat overrated song, 'The Exile of Erin,' which Campbell wrote after one evening finding Tony M'Cann more than usually depressed. Many years later an absurd claim to the authorship of this song was raised on behalf of an Irishman named Nugent, whose sister swore to having seen it in her brother's handwriting before the date of Campbell's continental visit. Campbell was naturally pained by the accusation, but he produced irrefragable proofs of his title to the song; and although the charge of plagiarism was revived after his death, there is not the slightest ground for doubting his authorship. The subject is fully dealt with by Beattie, but to discuss it nowadays would be altogether superfluous.

Before leaving home, Campbell had entered into an agreement with Mr Perry of the *Morning Chronicle* to send him something for his columns, and 'The Exile of Erin' was published by him on the 28th of January 1801. In a prefatory note the author expressed the hope that the song might induce Parliament to 'extend their benevolence to those unfortunate men, whom delusion and error have doomed to exile, but who sigh for a return to their native homes.' Campbell's sympathy with the Irish exiles appears to have been as strong as his sympathy with the Poles. He adopted as his seal a shamrock with the motto 'Erin-go-Bragh,' and his enthusiasm was so flamboyant that on his arrival in Edinburgh he was actually in some danger of being imprisoned for conspiring with General Moreau in Austria and with the Irish in Hamburg to land a French army in Ireland! Campbell might well be astonished at the idea of 'a boy like me' conspiring against the British Empire. Subsequently he made valiant efforts to obtain leave for M'Cann to return home. These efforts were unsuccessful, but he lived to see the exile established in Hamburg, through a fortunate marriage, as one of its wealthiest citizens.

During his residence at Altona, Campbell, when not engaged in composition, seems to have busied himself chiefly in trying to plumb the depths of German philosophy. He says—and he is 'almost ashamed to confess it'— that for twelve consecutive weeks he did nothing but study Kant. Distrusting his own imperfect acquaintance with German, he took a disciple of the master through his philosophy, but found nothing to reward the labour. His metaphysics, he remarked, were mere innovations upon the received meaning of words, and conveyed no more instruction than the writings of Duns Scotus or Thomas Aquinas. Of German philosophy in general Campbell entertained a very poor opinion. The language in his view was much richer in the field of *Belles Lettres*; and he claimed to have got more good from reading Schiller, Wieland, and Bürger than from any of the severer studies which he undertook at this time. Wieland he regarded with especial favour: he could not conceive 'a more perfect poet.' Of Goethe and Lessing, strangely enough, he makes practically no mention.

These details about Campbell's doings are gathered mainly from his letters to Richardson. He was still looking forward eagerly to the arrival of his friend; and when he wrote it was generally with the object of keeping his enthusiasm awake by glowing descriptions of Hungary, which he characterised as a 'poetical paradise,' the country 'worthy of our best research,' all the rest of Germany being only so much 'vulgar knowledge.' Campbell's well-laid schemes were, however, destined to be upset, and in a way which he evidently never anticipated. A great political crisis was at hand. England had determined to detach Denmark from the coalition by force of arms, and on the 12th of March the British fleet left Yarmouth Roads for the Sound. Altona being on the Danish shore was no longer eligible as a residence for English subjects, and Campbell, having already had more than enough of the pomp and circumstance of war, resolved to return home. He took a berth in the *Royal George*, bound for Leith, and the vessel dropped slowly down the river to Gluckstadt, in front of the Danish batteries. The passage proved very tedious, and in the end, instead of getting to Leith, the *Royal George* was spied by a Danish privateer and chased into Yarmouth. This was early in April, and on the 7th of the month Campbell arrived in London, where, through the good graces of Perry, he was at once made free of the best literary society of the day.

In connection with the continental sojourn thus hurriedly terminated, it remains now to consider the literary product of the nine months' absence from home. Like many another poet, Campbell will be remembered, if he is remembered at all, by his shorter pieces; and it is interesting to note that of these the best were written or at any rate conceived on alien soil. The 'Exile of Erin' has already been mentioned. 'Hohenlinden' did not appear until 1802, but there is every reason for believing that it was at least outlined shortly after the date of the occurrences which it so vividly pictures. Galt tells an amusing story of its rejection by a Greenock newspaper as not being 'up to the editor's standard'; but it took the fancy of Sir Walter Scott. When Washington Irving was at Abbotsford in 1817, Scott observed to him: 'And there's that glorious little poem, too, of "Hohenlinden"; after he [Campbell] had written it he did not seem to think much of it, but considered some of it d——d drum and trumpet lines. I got him to recite it to me, and I believe that the delight I felt and expressed had an effect in inducing him to print it.' The anecdote related by Scott in connection with Leyden is well-known. Campbell and Leyden, as we have seen, had quarrelled. When Scott repeated 'Hohenlinden' to Leyden, the latter said: 'Dash it, man, tell the fellow I hate him, but, dash it, he has written the finest verses that have been published these fifty years.' Scott did not fail to deliver the message. 'Tell Leyden,' said Campbell, 'that I detest him, but that I know the value of his critical approbation.'

Curiously enough, Carlyle, quoting in 1814 a poem of Leyden's on the victory of Wellington at Assaye, remarks that 'if there is anything in existence that surpasses this it must be "Hohenlinden"—but what's like "Hohenlinden"?' Leyden's verses in truth read somewhat tamely, but Carlyle's criticism of poetry was not to be depended upon, especially at this early date, when he preferred Campbell to either Byron or Scott. His impassioned liking for 'Hohenlinden' was, however, well justified by its merits. It has been described as the only representation of a modern battle which possesses either interest or sublimity. Sublimity is a word of which we are not particularly fond in these days, perhaps because it was so freely used by critics a hundred years ago. We prefer simplicity; and it is surely the simplicity of 'Hohenlinden' which mainly accounts for its effect. Each stanza is a picture—not a finished etching, but rather an 'impression'; no delicate shades of colour, but broad strokes of red and black on white. No word is wasted, no scene is elaborated; and if what is depicted is all pretty obvious—well, blood is red, and gunpowder is sulphurous, and there is little room for invention. To call it great art would be absurd; it is excellent scene-painting.

Next to 'Hohenlinden' among the pieces of this period must be placed 'Ye Mariners of England' and 'The Soldier's Dream.' The first was written at Altona when rumours of England's intention to break up the coalition began to spread. It was printed by Perry above the signature of 'Amator Patriæ,' with an intimation that it was avowedly an imitation of the seventeenth century sea-song, 'Ye Mariners of England,' which Campbell used to sing at musical soirees in Edinburgh. It is one of the most stirring of his war pieces. 'The Soldier's Dream,' beginning 'Our bugles sang truce,' was not given to the public until the spring of 1804, but it is generally believed to have been written at Altona, and in any case it was inspired by the events which the poet witnessed during his residence at Ratisbon. Several other pieces were composed or revised at this time, but they are of little importance. Byron declared that the 'Lines on leaving a Scene in Bavaria' were 'perfectly magnificent,' but the praise is grotesquely extravagant. The lines certainly bear traces of genuine feeling, but the piece as a whole is obscure and unfinished.

The famous 'Battle of the Baltic' was not published until 1809, but as it was suggested to Campbell by the sight of the Danish batteries as he sailed past them on his way home from Hamburg, it will be convenient to deal with it here. The subject of the poem is known in history as the Battle of Copenhagen, which was fought on the 2nd of April 1801. Campbell sent a first draft of it to Scott in 1805. This draft consisted of twenty-seven stanzas, while the published version has only eight. It has been remarked that if the original form had been adhered to, 'The Battle of the Baltic' might have become a popular ballad for a time and then been forgotten, whereas, in its condensed form, it is one of the finest and most enduring war-songs in the language. Its metre, which the *Edinburgh Review* thought 'strange and unfortunate,' is really one of its merits. The lines of unequal length relieve it of monotony; the sharp, short final line of each stanza being indeed an excellent invention. The poem has defects in plenty, which have been often enough pointed out: not a stanza would pass muster to-day; but it would be ungracious to criticise too severely one of the few vigorous battle pieces we have.

CHAPTER V
WANDERINGS—MARRIAGE—SETTLEMENT IN LONDON

During his sojourn on the Continent Campbell had suffered incredible hardships, hardships such as he hesitated to divulge even to his friends. Now he was to experience an agreeable change—a transition from 'the tedium of cold and gloomy evenings, unconsoled by the comforts of life, and from the barbarity of savages (where an Englishman was not sure of his life) to the elegant society of London and pleasures of every description.' He appears to have landed with little more than the Scotsman's proverbial half-crown in his pocket, but Perry, a Scot like himself, proved the friend in need. 'I will be all that you could wish me to be,' he said, and he kept his word. Calling upon him one day, Campbell was shown a letter from Lord Holland, inviting him to dine at the King of Clubs, a survival of the institution where Johnson used to lay down his little senate laws. 'Thither with his lordship,' says Campbell, writing in 1837, 'I accordingly repaired, and it was an era in my life. There I met, in all their glory and feather, Mackintosh, Rogers, the Smiths, Sydney, and others. In the retrospect of a long life I know no man whose acuteness of intellect gave me a higher idea of human nature than Mackintosh; and without disparaging his benevolence—for he had an excellent heart—I may say that I never saw a man who so reconciled me to hereditary aristocracy like the benignant Lord Holland.' Of Lady Holland, Campbell had an equally high opinion. She was, he said, a 'formidable woman, cleverer by several degrees than Buonaparte,' whose name, it is interesting to note, occurs again and again in his letters.

Among the other friends he made at this time were Dr Burney and Sir John Moore, Mrs Inchbald and Mrs Barbauld, J. P. Kemble, and Mrs Siddons. From a man so notoriously proud and reserved as Kemble he says he looked for little notice; but Kemble's behaviour at their first meeting undeceived him. 'He spoke with me in another room, and, with a grace more enchanting than the favour itself, presented me with the freedom of Drury Lane Theatre. His manner was so expressive of dignified benevolence that I thought myself transported to the identity of Horatio, with my friend Hamlet giving me a welcome.' Kemble's condescending kindness he ill-requited in 1817 with a set of wordy, inflated 'valedictory stanzas,' in which he displayed all his poetical apparatus of 'conscious bosoms,' 'classic dome,' 'supernal light,' and so forth. Mrs Siddons he describes as a woman of the first order, who sang some airs of her own composition with incomparable sweetness. In Rogers he found 'one of the most refined characters, whose manners and writing may be said to correspond.' Everybody and everything, in fact, delighted him; the pains of the past were forgotten, and the future began to look brighter than it had ever done before.

Unfortunately, just as he had got into this happy state of mind, he was startled by the news of his father's death. He had heard nothing of the old man's illness, and bitterly reproached himself for having left him in his last days. It was, however, some comfort to him to learn that Dr Anderson had watched at his bedside, and, when all was over, had seen his remains laid reverently in the cemetery of St John's Chapel. He died as he had lived, pious and placid, full of religious hope as of years. Campbell went home to console his mother and sisters, and to set their affairs in order. His father's annuity from the Glasgow Merchants' Society died with him; the sisters were good-looking but valetudinarian, and Campbell could only promise that if a new edition of 'The Pleasures of Hope' succeeded he would furnish a house in which they might keep boarders and teach school. Once in the house, he told them, they would have to trust in Providence.

The prospect certainly did not look promising, either for Campbell or his dependents. A thousand subscribers were required to make an edition of 'The Pleasures of Hope' safe and profitable, and as that number was not to be obtained in the north, Campbell was advised to go to London to canvass a larger public. Meanwhile he had to make both ends meet, and in default of precise information we must surmise that he turned out a deal of joyless, uncongenial work. Nor, with all his industry, did he succeed in relieving his straitened circumstances. The whole year was one of great privation, when the common necessaries of life were being sold at an exorbitant price, and 'meal-mob' rioters were parading the streets and breaking into the bakers' shops. People who had much more substantial resources than Campbell felt the temporary embarrassment. What Campbell should have done it would not be easy to say; what he did do it would be quite easy to censure. In spite of all his fine friends, for all the lavish promises of Perry and others, he was misguided enough to borrow money—on 'Judaic terms'—with, of course, the inevitable result. Beattie does not mention the sum borrowed, but he says it was nearly doubled by enormous interest, and could only be repaid by excessive application. Campbell was always notoriously careless in money matters, and even the concern he naturally felt as a devoted son and brother can hardly excuse the imprudence with which he added to his obligations at this period. But prudence, as Coleridge once pointed out, is not usually a plant of poetic growth.

In the midst of all his cares and anxieties, Campbell found some solace in the society of such literary and other friends as the Rev. Archibald Alison—the 'Man of Taste'—Professor Dugald Stewart, Lord Jeffrey, Dr Anderson, and the family of Grahames, of whom the author of 'The Sabbath' was the best known member. The fact of his having been at the seat of war gave his conversation a peculiar interest, and his pilgrimage generally was regarded as a subject of no little curiosity. His old pupil, Lord Cunninghame, remarks upon the change which his continental visit had evidently effected in his view of public affairs and the accepted order of things at home. Whatever youthful, hot-headed Republican notions he may have indulged before he went abroad, we gather that he had come back considerably sobered down, and now he deigned to express—he was still very young!—a decided preference for the British Constitution.

But literature was after all of more importance to him than politics. Such plans as he had formed at this time he freely discussed with Sir Walter Scott, from whom he received much encouragement and good advice. Lord Minto was another friend who proved of value. Minto had just returned from Vienna, where he had been acting as Envoy Extraordinary, and with the view perhaps of hearing his version of recent events in Germany, he invited the poet to his house at Castle Minto, some forty-five miles from Edinburgh. The visit turned out in every way agreeable, and when Campbell left, it was with the understanding that he would join Lord Minto in London in the course of the parliamentary session. A London visit promised many advantages, among them the opportunity of securing subscribers for the new edition of 'The Pleasures of Hope,' and Campbell returned to Edinburgh to make his preparations. He travelled overland, spending a few days in Liverpool with Currie, the biographer of Burns, and while there convulsing his friends by the nervousness he displayed on horseback. When he reached London he found that Minto had prepared a 'poet's room' for him at his house in Hanover Square, and there he took up his residence for the season, giving, it is understood, occasional service as secretary in return for the hospitality.

He says he found Minto's conversation very instructive, but Minto was a Tory of the Burke school, which Campbell regarded as inimical to political progress. Campbell naïvely remarks in one of his letters that at an early period of their acquaintance they had a discussion on the subject of politics, when he thought of giving Minto his political confession of faith. If it should not meet with Minto's approval, then the intimacy might end. Campbell does not appear to have rehearsed his whole political creed, but he went so far as to tell Minto that he was a Republican, and that his opinion of the practicability of a Republican form of government had not been materially affected by all that had happened in the French Revolution. Lord Minto was much too sensible a man to disturb himself about the political views of his overweening young guest, which, with a gentle sarcasm apparently unobserved by the poet, he set down as 'candid errors of judgment.' Still, there must have been some lively debates around the table now and again. The correspondence makes special mention of Touissant, the negro chieftain of San Domingo, as a subject of frequent wrangling. Campbell looked upon Touissant as a second

Kosciusko, while Minto could only dwell upon the horrors that were likely to follow upon his achievements in the cause of so-called freedom.

But these heated discussions were confined mainly to the morning hours. Campbell's chief concerns lay in other directions. Lord Minto left him very much master of his own time, and his literary friendships were now revived and extended at Perry's table, at the King of Clubs, and elsewhere. Minto introduced him to Wyndham, whom he describes as 'a Moloch among the fallen war-makers,' to Lord Malmesbury and Lord Pelham—'plain, affable men'—and to others. He met Malthus, whose theories he cordially supported, and found him 'most ingenious and pleasant, very sensible and good.' He was much flattered by the friendly notice of Mrs Siddons, and when the Kembles admitted him to their family circle, he announced in a burst of flunkeyism that he had attained the acme of his ambitions. With Telford the engineer, one of his Edinburgh patrons, and a genuine if not very judicious lover of poetry, he spent many of his leisure hours. Telford was intimate with the Secretary of State, and in one of his letters he hints to Alison that he may take some steps to direct the Minister's practical attention to the 'young Pope.'

Whether Telford carried out his intention does not appear; but at any rate there was no patronising of the young Pope, who continued to occupy his poet's room, and presently began to tell his friends in the north that he ardently longed to get away from his present scene of 'hurry and absurdity,' to the refined and select society of Edinburgh. Many young fellows in his position would have counted themselves lucky at being housed in such distinguished quarters; but Campbell was in a low state of health at the time, and that doubtless accounted for his aggravated fits of despondency. In any case he had his wish about returning to Edinburgh. At the close of the parliamentary session Minto started for Scotland, taking Campbell with him, and by the end of June he had exchanged his poet's room for the much humbler abode of his mother and sisters in Alison Square.

During this second visit to London he seems to have written very little, but what he did write has retained at least a certain school-book popularity. There was 'Hohenlinden,' finished at this time, and of which we have already spoken, and there was 'Lochiel's Warning,' a 'furious war prophecy,' in the composition of which he says he became greatly agitated and excited. 'Lochiel,' like 'Hohenlinden,' had been intended for the new edition of his poems, but, at the unexplained request of his friends, both pieces were printed anonymously and dedicated to Alison. Both had run the gauntlet of private criticism before being submitted to the public. When the rough draft of 'Lochiel' was handed to Minto—who with Currie and other friends criticised several successive drafts—he made some objection to the 'vulgarity' of hanging, and this objection was supported later on when the manuscript was passed about in Edinburgh. But Campbell was determined to show how his hero might swing with sufficient dignity in a good cause; and his objectors were silenced when he demonstrated to them that Lochiel had a brother who actually suffered death by means of the rope.

Of course his friends were not all so hypercritical as Minto. When he read 'Lochiel' to Mrs Dugald Stewart, she laid her hand on his head with the remark that it would bear another wreath of laurel yet. Campbell said this made a stronger impression upon him than if she had spoken in a strain of the loftiest laudation; nay, he declared it to have been one of the principal incidents in his life that gave him confidence in his own powers. Telford was even more enthusiastic. 'I am absolutely vain of Thomas Campbell,' he says in a letter to Alison. 'There never was anything like him—he is the very spirit of Parnassus. Have you seen his "Lochiel"? He will surpass everything ancient or modern—your Pindars, your Drydens, and your Grays. I expect nothing short of a Scotch Milton, a Shakespeare, or something more than either.'

To transcribe such stuff is really a tax on the biographer's patience. It was in this atmosphere of foolish adulation that Campbell spent those very years when a young man most needs the tonic air of rigorous criticism. Such coddling and cossetting never yet made a poet. Nothing that Campbell ever did justifies a panegyric like that just quoted; least of all is it justified by 'Lochiel's Warning,' a bit of first-rate fustian which would assuredly be forgotten but for its 'Coming events cast their shadows before,' and a certain rhetorical fluency, which—with its convenient length—make it a favourite with teachers of elocution. Campbell told Minto that he was tempted to throw the poem away in vexation at his inability to perfect it, and Scott himself had to insist on his retaining what were considered its finest lines. A writer, above all a poet, ought surely to *know*—as Tennyson, as Stevenson knew—when he has done a good thing; when he does *not* know, his friends are ill-advised in keeping his effusions from the flames. Scott, with his usual generosity, called the idea of the line quoted above a 'noble thought, nobly expressed.' The thought is Schiller's; and whatever 'nobility' there may be in the expression is spoilt in a great measure by the jingle of the first line of the couplet—

'Tis the sunset of life *gives me mystical lore.*

Even if this were not the case, its cachet of nobility could hardly survive the ridiculous story told by Beattie. Campbell, according to this circumstantial tale, was at Minto. He had gone early to bed and was reflecting on the

Wizard's warning when he fell asleep. During the night he suddenly awoke repeating: 'Events to come cast their shadows before.' It was the very image for which he had been waiting a week.

He rang the bell more than once with increased force. At last, surprised and annoyed by so unseasonable a peal, the servant appeared. The poet was sitting with one foot on the bed and the other on the floor, with an air of mixed impatience and inspiration. 'Sir, are you ill?' inquired the servant. 'Ill! never better in my life. Leave the candle and oblige me with a cup of tea as soon as possible.' He then started to his feet, seized hold of the pen, and wrote down the 'happy thought,' but as he wrote changed the words 'events to come' into 'coming events,' as it now stands in the text.

This is not exactly a case of *mons parturit murem*; it is more like the woman in the parable who beat up all her friends to rejoice with her in the discovery of her trinket; still more like the proud bantam who disturbs the whole neighbourhood for joy that a chick has been egged into the world. It would be difficult indeed to find a more striking example of much ado about nothing.

Sometime during the month of August Campbell had an intimation from Lord Minto that he was coming to Edinburgh, and would expect the poet to accompany him when he went south. Minto came, and Campbell left with him. In a letter to Scott Campbell says he must make the stay a short one, because he has arranged to take lessons in drawing from Nasmyth, but of that scheme nothing further is heard. Redding avers that Campbell could not use a pencil in the delineation of the simplest natural object, and instances an attempt to draw a cat which looked very like a crocodile. On the way to Minto the party halted at Melrose to allow Campbell to inspect the Abbey, with which he says he was pleased to enthusiasm. Scotland in the eleventh century, he exclaims sarcastically, could erect the Abbey of Melrose, and in the nineteenth could not finish the College of Edinburgh. He comments upon the fine, wild, yet light outline of its architecture, and says his mind was filled with romance at beholding 'in the very form and ornaments of the pile, proofs of its forest origin that lead us back to the darkest of Gothic ages.' When they arrived at Minto they were welcomed by Scott, among other visitors; and Campbell retired early to spend the evening with Hawkins' Life of Johnson, in which he found 'some valuable stuff in the midst of superabundant nonsense.'

On the whole, he does not seem to have been very happy at Minto during this visit. Lord Minto's politeness, he tells Alison, only twitches him with the sin of ingratitude for not being more contented under his hospitable roof. But a lord's house, fashionable strangers, luxuriously-furnished saloons, and winding galleries where he can hardly find his own room, make him as wretched as he can be, 'without being a *tutor.*' Everyone, it is true, treats him civilly; the servants are assiduous in setting him right when he loses his way; but degraded as he is to a state of second childhood in this 'new world,' it would be insulting his fallen dignity to smile hysterically and pretend to be happy. All of which is sheer fudge—nothing more than the splenetic utterance of an *enfant gaté.*

Happily, Campbell had business at home, and there was no reason why he should sit by the waters of Minto and sigh when he thought of Edinburgh. The new edition of his poems was now in the press, and he returned to the capital to revise the proofs. While he was thus engaged, other work of a less agreeable kind divided his attention. An Edinburgh bookseller had commissioned him to prepare 'The Annals of Great Britain,' a sort of continuation of Smollett, which he contracted to finish in three volumes octavo, at £100 per volume. The work was to be 'anonymous and consequently inglorious'—a labour, in fact, 'little superior to compilation, and more connected with profit than reputation.' It was a distinct drop for the author of 'The Pleasures of Hope,' and he knew it. Indeed, such was his sensitiveness on the point that he bound his employer to secrecy, and tried to hide the fact from even his most intimate friends. One cannot help comparing this behaviour with that of Tennyson; Campbell falling, even in his own estimation, below his very moderate level, deliberately doing work of which he was ashamed; Tennyson, perhaps going to the other extreme, sacrificing his worldly happiness and, it is to be feared, in part the health of the woman he loved, to the pursuit of his ideals. But Tennyson was a poet.

'The Annals of Great Britain' was not published until some years after this, but the book may be dismissed at once. It was little more than a dry catalogue of events chronologically arranged, a mere piece of journeyman's work done to turn a penny, without accuracy of information or the slightest regard for style. Campbell told Minto that the publisher did not desire that he should make the work more than passable, and it is barely passable. It is quite forgotten now; indeed, a writer in *Fraser's Magazine* for November 1844 declares that even then the most intelligent bookseller in London was unaware of its existence. Redding says that the author's own library was innocent of a copy.

While Campbell was hammering away at this perfunctory performance in Edinburgh, some whisper of honours and independence awaiting him in London seems to have reached his ears. It was only a whisper, but the time had clearly come when he must make up his mind once for all about the future. By his own admission, poetry had now deserted him; he had lost both the faculty and the inclination for writing it. Dull prose, he saw, must henceforward be his stand-by. As a market for dull prose, London undoubtedly ranked before Edinburgh; and so he took the plunge, though he had no fixed engagement in London, no actual business there except to superintend the printing of his poems. It was a bold venture, but in the end it probably turned out as well as any other venture would have done.

On the way south he was again the guest of Currie at Liverpool, where he remained 'drinking with this one and dining with that one' for ten days. Then he visited the pottery district of Staffordshire, where an old college friend was employed. It was his first real experience of the 'chaos of smoke,' and he did not like it. The country, he remarked, for all its furnaces, was not a 'hot-bed of letters,' though he had met with a character who enjoyed a reputation for learning by carrying a Greek Testament to church. The people were a heavy, plodding, unrefined race, but they had good hearts, and what was just as important, they gave good dinners. 'These honest folks showed me all the symptoms of their affection that could be represented by the symbols of meat and drink, and if ale, wine, bacon, and pudding could have made up a stranger's paradise I should have found it among the Potteries.' One untoward thing happened: Campbell lost his wig. For it should have been mentioned that just before he left Edinburgh, finding that his hair was getting alarmingly thin, he had adopted the peruke, which he continued to wear for the rest of his life. A bewigged poet of twenty-five must have been a somewhat singular spectacle in those days, but Campbell made up for the antiquated head-gear by a notable spruceness in other ways. He wore a blue coat with bright, gilt buttons, a white waistcoat and cravat, buff nankeens and white stockings, with shoes and silver buckles—a perfect scheme of colour.

In this gay attire, though 'agonised' by the want of his wig, he arrived in London on the 7th of March (1802). Telford at once took charge of him by making him his guest at the Salopian Hotel, Charing Cross. Of Telford's admiration for Campbell as a poet we have already learnt something; his opinion of Campbell as a man was apparently not quite so enthusiastic. Nothing is recorded of Campbell's conduct during the former visits to London, but what are we to infer from the fact that Telford and Alison now united to 'advise and remonstrate with the young poet, at a moment when he was again surrounded by all the seductive allurements of a great capital'? Alison sent him a letter of paternal counsel for the regulation of his life and studies; and Telford confided to Alison that he had asked Campbell to live with him in order to have him constantly in check. If Campbell really had any leaning towards social or other extravagances, it was promptly counteracted by an event of which we shall have to speak presently.

Meanwhile, Telford does not appear to have helped him much by introducing him to 'all sorts of novelty.' In fact, if we may believe himself, Campbell did not take at all kindly to London and its ways. Life there is 'absolutely a burning fever'; he hates its unnatural and crowded society; it robs him of both health and composure. He cannot settle himself to anything; he has one eternal round of invitations, and has got into a style of living which suits neither his purse nor his inclination. Sleep has become a stranger to him; every morning finds him with a headache. Study and composition are out of the question. He sits 'under the ear-crashing influence of ten thousand chariot wheels'; when night comes on he has no solace but his pipe, and he drops into bed like an old sinner dropping into the grave.

Campbell was very likely homesick, but his correspondence and the evidence of his intimates put it beyond doubt that he was not cut out for society. Indeed he expressly admits it himself. Fashionable folks, he exclaims in one of his letters, have a slang of talk among themselves as unintelligible to ordinary mortals as the lingo of the gipsies, and perhaps not so amusing if one did understand it. A man of his lowly breeding feels in their company something of what Burke calls proud humility, or rather humble contempt. As for conversation with these minions of *le beau monde*, he says it is not worth courting since their minds are not so much filled as dilated. This was another of Campbell's many foolish utterances of the kind. It must have been made in a fit of spleen, for Campbell, like Burns, could dinner very comfortably with a lord when the meeting was likely to favour his own interests.

Johnson declared of Charing Cross that the full tide of human existence was there, but Campbell had nothing of Johnson's affection for the streets. He objected to the noise because it made conversation impossible, or at least difficult. Hence it was that, 'the roaring vortex' having proved unendurable to him, he now changed his quarters to a dingy den of his own at 61 South Molton Street. Here he went on preparing the 'Annals' and the new edition of his poems, toiling with the stolid regularity of the mill-horse for ten hours a day. The new edition of the poems was published in the beginning of June, when his spirits had sunk to 'the very ground-floor of despondency.' It was a handsome quarto, and the printing, in the author's opinion, was so well done that, except one splendid book from Paris, dedicated to 'that villain Buonaparte,' there was nothing finer in Europe. It was really the seventh edition of 'The Pleasures of Hope,' but it contained several engravings and some altogether new pieces, among which, in addition to 'Lochiel' and 'Hohenlinden,' were the once bepraised 'Lines on Visiting a Scene in Argyllshire' (the old family estate of Kirnan), and 'The Beech Tree's Petition.'

In the course of some pleasantry at the house of Rogers, Campbell once remarked that marriage in nine cases out of ten looks like madness. His own case was clearly not the tenth, at any rate from a prudential point of view. The sale of his new volume had given a temporary fillip to his exchequer, and with the proverbial rashness of his class, he began to think of taking a wife. His reasons were certainly more substantial than his finances. He says that without a home of his own he found it impossible to keep to his work. When he lived alone in lodgings he became so melancholy that for whole days together he did nothing, and could not even stir out of doors. In the company of a certain lady he had found for the first time in his life a 'perpetual serenity of mind,' and now he was determined to hazard everything for such a prize. It was a big hazard, and he foresaw the objections. His infatuation, he remarks to Currie, will inevitably set many an empty head a-shaking. But happiness and prosperity do not, in his view, depend upon frigid maxims; and the strong motive he will now have to exertion he regards as 'worth uncounted thousands' for encountering the ills of existence.

The lady for whom Campbell thus braved the uncertain future was a daughter of his maternal cousin, Mr Robert Sinclair, who had been a wealthy Greenock merchant and magistrate, and was now, after having suffered some financial reverses, living retired in London. She bore 'the romantic name of Matilda,' and is described by Campbell as a beautiful, lively, and lady-like woman, who could make the best cup of Mocha in the world. Beattie remarks upon the Spanish cast of her features: her complexion was dark, her figure spare, graceful, and below the middle height, and when she smiled her eyes gave an expression of tender melancholy to her face. Like Campbell, she had been abroad, and it is said that at the Paris Opera she attracted great attention in her favourite head-dress of turban and feathers. The Turkish Ambassador, who was in a neighbouring box, declared that he had seen nothing so beautiful in Europe. We have learned that Campbell himself was handsome, but Mr Sinclair naturally did not regard good looks as a guarantee of an assured income, and he stoutly opposed the match. The prospective husband was not, however, to be put off by talk about the precarious profits of literature. When was he likely to be in a better position to marry? He had few or no debts; the subscriptions to his quarto were still coming in; the 'Annals' was to bring him £300; and at that very moment he had a fifty pound note in his desk.

Mr Sinclair remained unmoved by this recital of wealth, but finding that his daughter's health was suffering, he waived his objections, and arrangements were made for the marriage to take place at once. Campbell now adopted every means in his power to make money. He wrote to his friend Richardson, requesting him to take prompt measures for levying contributions among the Edinburgh booksellers, the stockholders of the new edition. 'In the name of Providence,' he demands in desperation, 'how much can you scrape out of my books in Edinburgh? If you can dispose of a hundred volumes at fifteen shillings each, it will raise me £75. I shall require £25 to bring me down to Scotland ... and under £50 I cannot furnish a house, which, at all events, I am determined to do.' This request was made only nine days before the marriage, which was celebrated at St Margaret's, Westminster, on the 10th of October 1803—not September, as Beattie and Campbell himself have it. After a short honeymoon trip, the pair returned to town and settled down in Pimlico, where the father-in-law had considerately furnished a suite of rooms for them.

Campbell's idea had been to make his home in some 'cottage retreat' near Edinburgh. He did not want society or callers; he wanted to be sober and industrious; therefore he would live in the country if he should have to go ten miles in search of a box. He dwells lovingly on this prospect in letters to his friends; but although he did not abandon the notion for some time, it never came to anything. As a matter of fact, his new responsibilities led to engagements which practically chained him to London; to say nothing of the circumstance that he had joined the Volunteers, in view of the threatened invasion of which he sung. Moreover, he had got into some trouble with his Edinburgh publisher, and probably he felt that his presence in or near the capital would only add to his personal annoyance. How different his after life might have been had he carried out his original intention, it is useless to speculate.

As it was, he had not been long married when financial difficulties began to bear heavily upon him. He started badly by borrowing money from one of his sisters; later on he borrowed £55 from Currie; and finally he had to ask a loan of £50 from Scott. A man of really independent spirit, such as Campbell professed to be, would have felt all this very galling, but there is nothing to indicate that Campbell experienced more than a momentary sense of shame at the position in which he had placed himself. By and by we find him confessing to Currie that he doubted whether he had ever been a poet at all, so grovelling and so parsimonious had he become: 'I have grown a great scrub, you would hardly believe how avaricious.' To explain the necessity for these unpoetic borrowings would be somewhat difficult. It certainly did not arise from idleness or want of work. Campbell was constantly being offered literary employment, and he had by this time formed a profitable engagement with *The Star*. In November he describes himself as an exceedingly busy man, habitually contented, and working twelve hours a day for those depending on him. 'I am scribble, scribble, scribbling for that monosyllable which cannot be wanted—bread, not fame.' But the scribbling, it may be presumed, did not furnish him with much ready cash, and the current household expenses had to be provided for. By this time there were debts, too. Bensley, the printer, pressed him for a bill of £100; he owed one bookseller £30, and he had an account of £25 for his Volunteer uniform and accoutrements, which were to have cost originally only £10.

Campbell seldom writes a letter without referring to these sordid concerns; but, on the other hand, he just as often speaks of his newly-found felicity by his own fireside. Never, he says, did a more contented couple sit in their Lilliputian parlour. Matilda sews beside him all day, and except to receive such visitors as cannot be denied, they remain without interruption at their respective tasks. In course of time the Lilliputian parlour was brightened by a new arrival. The poet's first child, Thomas Telford—so called in compliment to the engineer, who afterwards paid for it in a handsome legacy—was born on July 1st, 1804. In notifying Currie of the event he grows quite eloquent over the 'little inestimable accession' to his happiness, and asserts his belief that 'lovelier babe was never smiled upon by the light of heaven.' In view of what occurred later, the following reads somewhat pathetically: 'Oh that I were sure he would live to the days when I could take him on my knee and feel the strong plumpness of childhood waxing into vigorous youth! My poor boy! shall I have the ecstacy of teaching him thoughts, and knowledge, and reciprocity of love to me? It is bold to venture into futurity so far. At present his lovely little face is a comfort to me.' Well was it for Thomas Campbell that the future of his boy lay only in his imagination!

In the meantime, having begun to give hostages to fortune, he felt that he must make still greater efforts towards securing a settled income. This year he had been offered a lucrative professorship in the University of Wilna, but although he declared his readiness to take any situation that offered certain support, he hesitated about the offer because of the decided way in which he had spoken against Russia in 'The Pleasures of Hope.' He had no fancy for being sent to Siberia, and so, after carefully considering the matter, he declined to go to Wilna. It was at this time that, under the feeling of his responsibility as a parent, he conceived the idea of his 'Specimens of the British Poets.' He desired to haul in from the bookselling tribe as many engagements as possible, of such a kind as would cost little labour and bring in a big profit. The 'Specimens,' he thought, would answer to that description; and he suggests to Currie that some Liverpool bookseller might embark £500 in the undertaking and make £1000. Find the man, he says, in effect, to Currie. Although Currie should ruin him by the undertaking, it would only be ruining a bookseller, and doing a benefit to a friend! That was one way in which Campbell proposed to meet his increased responsibilities. Another way was by removing his residence to the suburbs. At Pimlico, visitors, as he expresses it, haunted him like fiends and ate up his time like moths. To escape them, as well as to be out of the reach of 'family interference' (this was rather ungracious after the father-in-law's furnishing!), he took a house at Sydenham, and in the November of 1804 he was 'safe at last in his *dulce domum*.'

CHAPTER VI
POETICAL WORK AND PROSE BOOKMAKING

In 1804 Sydenham was a country village so primitive in its arrangements that its water was brought on carts, and cost two shillings a barrel. It had a common upon which the matter-of-fact Matilda thought she might keep pigs, and a lovely country, still untouched by the hand of the jerry-builder, lay all around it. 'I have,' says Campbell, describing his situation, 'a whole field to expatiate over undisturbed: none of your hedged roads and London out-of-town villages about me, but "ample space (*sic*) and verge enough" to compose a whole tragedy unmolested.' The house, which he had leased for twenty-one years at an annual rent of forty guineas, consisted of six rooms, with an attic storey which he converted into a working 'den' for himself. Altogether it was a charming home for a literary man, and Campbell ought to have been contented and happy. His London friends came to see him on Sundays, and among his neighbours he found many sincere friends, notwithstanding Lockhart's superfine sneers about 'suburban blue-stockings, weary wives, idle widows, and involuntary nuns.'

Unhappily, the old moodiness and discontent returned upon him. He had work, but work which he despised. He was fairly paid, but though Mrs Campbell was a 'notable economist,' there was always apparently some difficulty in getting the financial belt to meet. Campbell himself was, as we have learned, hopelessly incapable in money matters; indeed, he affirmed that he was usually ready to shoot himself when he came to the subject of cash accounts. He had settled at Sydenham with his nose just above water. Currie had advanced him £55, and Gregory Watt, his early college friend, who died about this time, had left him a legacy of £100; but the furnishing and the flitting had swallowed it all up, and a 'Judaic loan' besides. His main source of income at this date was from the quarto edition of his poems, and the sale of that was beginning to flag. It is true he had his four guineas a week from the *Star*; but out of this he had to pay for a conveyance to take him to town daily. We must remember, besides, that he had two establishments to provide for, his mother's at Edinburgh, as well as his own at Sydenham; and in those times, when war prices ruled, the cost of living was excessively high. But all this does not quite explain the perpetual trouble about money—does not explain how it should have been necessary for Lady Holland to send a 'munificent present' to save him from a debtor's lodging in the King's Bench.

Campbell was not the man to bear poverty in uncomplaining silence. His letters of this period are filled with plaints, whinings, regrets, implicit accusations against Providence of dealing unfairly with one who had been made for so much better things. He chafes at the necessity for yoking himself to the irksome tasks of the literary drudge, tasks that require little more than the labour of penmanship. He deplores that his Helicon has dried up; he has no poetry in his brain, he tells Scott, and inspiration is a stranger to him from extreme apprehension about the future. The only art now left to him, he sadly confesses, is the art of sitting for so many hours a day at his desk.

The result of all this work and worry and disappointment was soon seen on his health. His anxiety to be up in the morning kept him awake at night, and he became a victim to insomnia. He sought relief in laudanum, which, while procuring him sleep, only increased his constitutional tendency to mope. He began to think he was dying, and even wished himself dead. There is something, he remarked to Richardson in 1805, in one's internal sensations that tells more certainly of disorder than the diagnosis of the doctors, and those sensations he was undoubtedly conscious of feeling. The thought of the consummation comforted him rather than otherwise, though he shuddered at the 'dreadful and melancholy idea' of leaving his wife and family unprovided for—'as it is not impossible they may soon be.' Of course things were not nearly so bad as this. Campbell was certainly not well, and his financial affairs, thanks mainly to his own mismanagement, were not in a prosperous state; but his ailments and embarrassments were clearly aggravated by his morbid imagination. It was nothing more serious than a case of liver and *amour propre*. If, like Scott after the great crash, he had cheerfully and resolutely confronted his circumstances, the ailments and embarrassments, if they had not vanished entirely, would infallibly have assumed a less threatening aspect. But that, after all, is only to say that Thomas Campbell should have been—not Thomas Campbell but somebody else.

He would require to be indeed an enthusiastic biographer who should write with any zest of Campbell's literary labours during these years. Great writers have often enough been great hacks, but seldom has a man of Campbell's poetical promise descended to such dull drudgery as that to which he had now betaken himself. He continued to toil at the 'Annals'; he wrote papers for the *Philosophical Magazine*, he translated foreign correspondence for the *Star*, and, in brief, gave himself up almost entirely to the 'inglorious employment' of anonymous writing and compilation. He wrote on every imaginable subject, including even agriculture, on the knowledge of which he says he was more than once complimented by farmers, though Lockhart cruelly remarks that he probably could not tell barley from lavender. Politics, too, he tried, but therein was found wanting. He had no real acquaintance with the political questions of the time, nor did he possess the journalistic faculty in any degree. Before he finally left the *Morning Chronicle*, his connection with which had continued, he was doing little but writing pieces to fill up the poets' corner, and even these were sometimes so poor that Perry declined to insert them.

What Campbell always wanted—what indeed he made no secret of wanting—was some project which would mean light labour and long returns. Early in 1806 he had become acquainted with John Murray, the publisher, at whose literary parties he was afterwards a frequent guest, and the possibilities of the connection had at once presented themselves. The first hint of these possibilities is revealed in some correspondence which now took place about a new journal that Murray evidently intended Campbell to edit. The details of the scheme were being discussed when there was some talk about an *Athenæum* being started, and Campbell pleads with Murray not to be discouraged by the beat of the rival's drum. 'Supposing,' he exclaims, 'we had an hundred *Athenæums* to confront us, is it not worth our while to make a great effort?' The correspondence certainly shows that Campbell was anxious enough to make the effort; but the proposal dropped entirely out of sight, and he had to set his brains to work in the evolution of other schemes.

Several ideas occurred to him. He thought of translating a 'tolerable poem,' French or German, of from six to ten thousand lines, and he begged Scott to advise him about the choice. He cogitated upon a collection of Irish music, but found that Moore had anticipated him. He had considerable correspondence with Scott and others about the proposed 'Specimens of the British Poets,' in which project Scott and he had, unknown to each other, coincided, but that too had to be given up, at any rate for the present. This scheme, as Lockhart tells us, was first suggested by Scott to Constable, who heartily supported it. By and by it was discovered that Cadell & Davies and some other London publishers had a similar plan on foot, and were now, after having failed with Sir James Mackintosh, negotiating with Campbell about the biographical introductions. Scott proposed that the Edinburgh and London houses should join hands in the venture, and that the editorial duties should be divided between himself and Campbell. To this both Cadell and Campbell readily assented, but the design as originally sketched ultimately fell to the ground, because the booksellers declined to admit certain works upon which the editors insisted.

Such, in brief, is the history of the undertaking which was to have united in one 'superb work' the names of Scott and Campbell. It is unnecessary to dwell further on it, unless, perhaps, to note that Campbell's notoriously rabid opinions of publishers seem to have had their origin in the negotiations. Everybody has heard how he once toasted Napoleon because he had ordered a bookseller to be shot! The booksellers, he remarks to Scott, are the greatest ravens on earth, liberal enough as booksellers go, but still 'ravens, croakers, suckers of innocent blood and living men's brains.' They 'pledge one another in authors' skulls, the publisher always taking the lion's share.' Dependence upon these 'cunning ones' he finds to be so humiliating—they are so prone to insult all but the prosperous and independent—that he secretly determines to have in future as little to do with them as possible. He is no match for them: they know the low state of his finances, and take advantage of him accordingly. Murray is 'a very excellent and gentleman-like man—albeit a bookseller—the only gentleman, except Constable, in the trade.' And much more to the same effect. There was really nothing in the correspondence about the 'Specimens' which should have led Campbell thus to traduce a body of men upon whom he was so dependent, and by whom, with hardly a single exception, he was always honourably and even generously treated. He asked too much for his work—£1000 was his figure—the booksellers thought they could not afford so much, and they said so. It was Campbell himself who was at fault. He took absurdly high ground—boasted, in fact, of taking high ground—and talked of £1000 as quite a perquisite. In short, he had as little personal justification for libelling the booksellers as Byron had for comparing them with Barabbas.

Defeated in his design for the British poets, Campbell now went about whimpering that he had no hopes of an agreeable undertaking, unless Scott could hit upon some plan which would admit of their joining hands in the editorship. Longman & Rees had engaged him to edit a small collection of specimens of Scottish poetry, with a glossary and notices of two or three lives, but that he regarded as 'a most pitiful thing.' Scott had no suggestion to make, and Campbell, fretting over his prospects and his frustrated hopes—or as Beattie hints, neglecting his food—again fell ill. A second son, whom he named Alison, after his old Edinburgh friend, had been born to him in June 1805, but the jubilation over the event was short-lived. He became, in fact, more moody and disconsolate than ever. He described himself as a wreck, and looked forward to his sleepless nights being 'quieted soon and everlastingly.' Even the daily journey to town proved too much for him, and he took a temporary lodging in Pimlico, going to Sydenham only on Sundays. By and by he recovered himself a little. Medical skill did something, but improved finances did more. In a letter to Scott, dated October 2, 1805, we find this curt but pregnant postscript: 'His Majesty has been pleased to confer a pension of £200 a year upon me. GOD SAVE THE KING.' Campbell says the 'bountiful allowance' was obtained through several influences, but he mentions Charles Fox (who liked him because he was 'so right about Virgil'), Lord Holland and Lord Minto as being specially active in the matter.

It was insinuated that the pension came as a reward for writing a series of newspaper articles in defence of the Grenville administration, but this was certainly not the case. Campbell was no political writer, no 'scribbler for a party.' Among his many faults it cannot be laid to his charge that he sold his principles for pay. In 1824, mercenary as he was, he declined £100 a year from a certain society because to take the money meant 'canting and time-serving.' We need therefore have no hesitation in accepting his assurance that he received the present grant 'purely and exclusively as an act of literary patronage.' There is perhaps a suspicion of the *poseur* in his palaver about the 'mortification' which his pride had suffered in the matter, but beyond that, there seems to be no reason for casting doubts on his political honesty.

The new accession of fortune was not princely, but it must have helped Campbell very considerably. Deducting office fees, duties, etc., the allowance amounted to something like £168 per annum, and that sum he enjoyed for close upon forty years. He says that his physicians—who were surely Job's comforters all—told him he must regard it as the only barrier between him and premature dissolution; and he speaks about making it 'do' in the cheapest corner of England. His friends, however, were by this time thoroughly alive to the necessity, which indeed should never have existed, of doing something to put his finances on a satisfactory basis, and to this end the publication of another subscription edition of his poems was arranged. Campbell indulged in his usual idle talk about 'mortification' at having again to ask support in this way, but his friends wisely kept the matter in their own hands and paid no heed to his maunderings.

At the same time some impatience was not unnaturally being felt with Campbell. Francis Horner, a judicious acquaintance upon whom he afterwards wrote an unfinished elegy, was giving himself no end of trouble over the new edition, and this is the way he writes to Richardson. Speaking of a permanent fund as a motive to economy he says:

You must teach him [Campbell] to consider this subscription as an exertion which cannot with propriety, nor even perhaps with success, be tried another time; and that from this time he must look forward to a plan of income and expense wholly depending upon himself and most strictly adjusted. He gets four guineas a week for translating foreign gazettes at the *Star* office; it is not quite the best employment for a man of genius, but it occupies him only four hours of the morning, and the payment ought to go a great length in defraying his annual expenses. You will be able to convey to Campbell these views of his situation and others that will easily occur to you: none of *us* are entitled to use so much freedom with him.

One can read a good deal between the lines here. Campbell, as he mildly puts it himself, was never 'over head and ears in love with working'; he preferred his friends to work for him. Some years before this he looked to them to get him a Government situation, 'unshackled by conditional service'; and even now, with his pension running, and much as he prated about his pride, he 'trusts in God' that it will be followed up by an appointment of 'some emolument' in one of the Government offices. It was clearly an object with him to have his affairs made easy by outsiders. Nor was this all. There is no doubt that he had, temporarily at least, given way to convivial habits which his well-wishers could not but regard with regret. He admits as much himself, and Beattie only seeks to hide the fact by speaking in his solemn, periphrastic way about 'the social pleasures of the evening' and a 'too-easy compliance' with the solicitations of company. In these circumstances, it was only natural that Campbell's friends should desire to impress upon him the necessity of guiding his affairs with greater circumspection so as to depend more upon himself. Meanwhile they went on collecting subscribers' names for the new edition, and Campbell returned to Sydenham to continue his work on the 'Annals' and think about something less irksome and more remunerative.

It was at this juncture that Murray considerately came to his aid. Though the original scheme of the British Poets had fallen through, Campbell had by no means given up the idea of a work of the kind; and now, having discussed the plan with Murray, it was arranged between them that the undertaking should go on. Murray was naturally anxious that Scott's name should be connected with the editorship, but Scott, although he at first agreed to co-operate, ultimately found it necessary to restrict himself to works more exclusively his own, and Campbell was accordingly left to proceed alone.

In the summer of 1807 his labours were interrupted by a visit to the Isle of Wight. His old complaint had returned, and he was advised to try a change of air and scene. He left London in the beginning of June, but the change did not prove successful. The demon of insomnia still haunted him, and the *ennui* of the place became so intolerable that he was driven to act as reader to the ladies in the boarding-house where he stayed! What, he cries, must Siberia be when Ryde is so bad! By August he was at Sydenham again, only to find his 'abhorred sleeplessness returning fast and inveterately.' He had written very little poetry for some time, and such as he did write—the tribute to Sir John Moore, for example—is, like the Greek mentioned by Pallet, not worth repeating. He was now engaged almost solely upon 'Gertrude of Wyoming,' but his head was 'constantly confused,' and the poem was often laid aside for weeks at a time. Still, the manuscript advanced, and by Christmas the greater part of it was complete enough for reading to a private circle of friends.

'Gertrude' finally appeared, after a long process of polishing, alteration and addition, in April 1809. Some time before its publication Campbell wrote that he had no fear as to its reception; only let him have it out, and, like Sterne, he cared not a curse what the critics might say. The critics were in the main favourable. Jeffrey had already seen the proofs, and had written a long letter to the author, pointing out certain 'dangerous faults,' but commending the poem for its 'great beauty and great tenderness and fancy'; and on the same day that the poem was published, the *Edinburgh Review* appeared with an article in which the editor rejoiced 'once more to see a polished and pathetic poem in the old style of English pathos and poetry.' Its merits, he said, 'consist chiefly in the feeling and tenderness of the whole delineation, and the taste and delicacy with which all the subordinate parts are made to contribute to the general effect.' At the same time he found the story confused, some passages were unintelligible, and there was a laborious effort at emphasis and condensation which had led to 'constraint and obscurity of the diction.' The *Quarterly* reviewer, none other than Sir Walter Scott, was more severe upon its blemishes. He complained of the 'indistinctness' of the narrative, of the numerous blanks which were left to be filled up by the imagination of the reader, of its occasional ambiguity and abruptness. Its excellences were, however, generously admitted; and in fact, on the whole, the *Quarterly* said as much in its favour as could be expected. In those days party spirit led to incredible freaks of literary criticism; and it was only Scott's magnanimity that could have allowed him to forgive Campbell's Whig politics for the sake of his poetry. Curiously enough, considering their intimacy, Campbell did not know that Scott was his reviewer, though he was not very wide of the mark when he spoke of the writer as 'a candid and sensible man,' who 'reviews like a gentleman, a Christian, and a scholar.' Of other contemporary criticisms we need not speak. The poet's friends were of course blindly eulogistic. Alison was 'delighted and conquered,' and Telford, with his characteristic bombast, anticipated such applause from the public as would drive the author frantic!

'Gertrude,' as has more than once been pointed out, was the first poem of any length by a British writer the scene of which was laid in America, and in it Campbell is the first European to introduce his readers to the romance of the virgin forests and Red Indian warriors. The subject may have occurred to him when transcribing a passage in his own 'Annals,' in which reference is made to the massacre of Wyoming, although there is possibly something in Beattie's suggestion that he got the idea from reading Lafontaine's story of 'Barneck and Saldorf,' published in 1804. Campbell, however, as we know, had a keen personal interest in America. His father had lived there; three of his brothers were there now. 'If I were not a Scotsman,' he once remarked, 'I should like to be an American.' No doubt the scenery of Pennsylvania had been often described to him in letters from the other side.

But these are points that do not greatly concern us now. Nor is it necessary to enter into any minute criticism of the poem. Campbell himself preferred it to 'The Pleasures of Hope' ('I mean,' he said, 'to ground my claims to future notice on it'), while Hazlitt regarded it as his 'principal performance.' With neither opinion does the popular verdict agree. Perhaps it may be that while 'Gertrude' is, as Lockhart said, a more equal and better sustained effort than 'The Pleasures of Hope,' it contains fewer passages which bear detaching from the context. For one thing the poet had a story to tell in 'Gertrude,' and he was eminently unskilled in the management of poetic narrative. 'I was always,' he remarks to Scott, 'a dead bad hand at telling a story.' In 'Gertrude' he cannot keep to his story; the construction of the entire poem is loose and incoherent. Even the love scenes, which, as Hazlitt says, breathe a balmy voluptuousness of sentiment, are generally broken off in the middle. Then he was unwise in adopting the Spenserian stanza. It was quite alien to his style; even Thomson, living long before the romantic revival, managed it more sympathetically than Campbell. The necessities of the rhyme led Campbell to invert his sentences unduly, to tag his lines for the mere sake of the rhyme, and to use affected archaisms with a quite extraordinary clumsiness. Anything more unlike the sweet, easy, graceful compactness of Spenser could scarcely be imagined.

Nor are the characters of the poem altogether successful; indeed, with the single exception of the Indian, they are mere shadows. Gertrude herself makes a pretty portrait; but as Hazlitt has remarked, she cannot for a moment compare with Wordsworth's Ruth, the true infant of the woods and child-nature. Brant, again, who so warmly espoused the cause of the Mohawks during the War of the American Revolution, is but a faint reality. Campbell fancied that he had drawn a true picture of the partisan, but as Brant's son afterwards proved to him, the picture was purely imaginary. The main function of the Indian chief is apparently to give local colour to the poem, though it must be allowed that he stands out boldly among its other characters. Hazlitt comments upon his erratic appearances, remarking that he vanishes and comes back, after long intervals, in the nick of time, without any known reason but the convenience of the author and the astonishment of the reader. On the other hand, the death-song of the savage which closes the poem, is one of the best things that the author ever wrote.

Byron declared that 'Gertrude' was notoriously full of grossly false scenery; that it had 'no more locality with Pennsylvania than with Penmanmaur.' But that was an obvious exaggeration. There is better ground for the complaint about Campbell's errors in natural history as exhibited in the poem—about his having conferred on Pennsylvania the aloe and the palm, the flamingo and the panther. The probability is that he knew as much about natural history as Goldsmith, whose friends declared that he could not tell the difference between any two sorts of barndoor fowl until they had been cooked. Once in the *New Monthly*, when a contributor spoke of the rarity of seeing the cuckoo, Campbell added a correcting note to say that he had himself 'seen whole fields *blue* with cuckoos'! But even Shakespeare has lions in the forest of Arden, and Goldsmith makes the tiger howl in North America. There is no need to insist upon absolute accuracy in such matters. One would gladly notice instead the real merits of the poem, which, however, are not so readily discovered. Hazlitt spoke enthusiastically of passages of so rare and ripe a beauty that they exceed all praise. But we have changed our poetical point of view since Hazlitt's day; and the most that can now be said for 'Gertrude,' is that it is a third-rate poem containing a few first-rate lines. It is practically dead, and can never be called back to life.

'Gertrude' was favourably received by the public, and particularly by the Whig party, to whose leaders Campbell was personally known, and with most of whom he was closely intimate. It was edited in America by Washington Irving in 1810, and was highly praised on the other side—a fact which at least suggests that its local scenery was not so false as Byron declared it to be. The first edition was a quarto; a second in 12mo was called for within the year. The quarto edition included some of the better known short pieces, such as 'Ye Mariners,' 'The Battle of the Baltic,' 'Lochiel,' 'Lord Ullin's Daughter,' and 'Glenara,' the latter founded on a wild and romantic story of which Joanna Baillie afterwards made use in her 'Family Legend.' The second edition contained the once-familiar 'O'Connor's Child,' a rather touching piece suggested by the flower popularly known as 'Love Lies Bleeding.' Many years after this—in 1836—the Dublin people desired to give Campbell a public dinner as the author of 'O'Connor's Child' and 'The Exile of Erin,' but Campbell never set foot on the Emerald Isle.

CHAPTER VII
LECTURES AND TRAVELS

Having got 'Gertrude' off his hands, Campbell returned to his literary carpentering. He was now in his thirty-third year, and had produced the two long poems and the short pieces upon which his fame, such as it is, rests. Were it not for his lines on 'The Last Man,' it would have been much better for his reputation had he never again put pen to paper. It was a remark of Scott's that he had broken out at once, like the Irish rebels, a hundred thousand strong. But unfortunately he had no sustaining power; he could not keep up the attack. His imaginative faculty, never robust, decayed much earlier than that of any other poet who ever gave like promise; and we have the sorry spectacle of a man still under forty living in the shadow of a reputation made when he was little more than out of his teens.

One says it regretfully, but it is the sober truth that Campbell became now a greater hack than ever. He declared in the frankest possible manner that he did not mean to think of poetry any more; he meant to make money, a desire which was very near his heart all along. He had been working fourteen hours a day for some time, but the weak flesh began to complain, and four hours had to be cut off. In 1810 he lost his youngest child, Alison, and overwhelmed himself with grief. Before he had recovered from the shock his mother passed away in Edinburgh. She had been suffering from paralysis, and so far as we can learn Campbell had nothing more touching to say of her death than to express his 'sincere acquiescence' in the dispensation of Providence.

One or two little incidents helped to revive his spirits after the snapping of these sacred ties. He had been presented to the Princess of Wales by Lady Charlotte Campbell, who thoughtfully, as he tells a correspondent—but why thoughtfully?—kept the Princess from making an 'irruption' into his house. The Princess summoned him to Blackheath, where he had the felicity of dancing a reel with her, and thus 'attained the summit of human elevation.' An onlooker remarked upon this performance that Campbell had 'the neat national trip,' but we have no other evidence of his dancing accomplishments. Campbell was delighted with himself; but he soon discovered that his good luck in making a royal acquaintance might prove embarrassing. He had unthinkingly remarked to the Princess that he loved operas to distraction. 'Then why don't you go to them?' she inquired. Campbell made some excuse about the expense, and next day a ticket for the season arrived. 'God help me!' he says, in recounting the incident, 'this *is* loving operas to distraction. I shall be obliged to live in London a month to attend the opera-house—all for telling one little fib.'

As a matter of fact, Campbell had now something more serious to think about than attending the Opera. He had been engaged, at his own suggestion, to give a course of lectures on Poetry at the Royal Institution, the fee to be one hundred guineas for the course. When Scott heard of the undertaking he expressed the hope that Campbell would read with fire and feeling, and not attempt to correct his Scots accent. But Campbell did not agree with Scott on the latter point. He tells Alison that he has taken great pains with his voice and pronunciation, and has laboured hard to get rid of his Caledonianisms. Sydney Smith, he says, patronised him more than he liked about the lectures, and gave him what, in Campbell's case, was clearly a wise hint against joking. In truth he seems to have had more than enough of advice from his friends, but he went his own way, and he was amply justified by the result.

The first lecture, delivered on the 24th of April 1812, proved a great success. According to a contemporary account, the hall was crowded, and the 'eloquent illustrations' of the lecturer received the warmest praise. Campbell says his own expectations were more than realised, though he had been so far from a state of composure that he playfully threatened to divorce his wife if she attended! At the close of the lecture distinguished listeners pressed around him with compliments. 'Byron, who has now come out so splendidly, told me he heard Bland the poet say, "I have had more *portable* ideas given me in the last quarter of an hour than I ever imbibed in the same portion of time." Archdeacon Nares fidgetted about and said: "that's new; at least quite new to *me*."' And so on. Campbell's friends were less critical than kind. The modern reader of his lectures will not find anything so new as Nares found, nor anything so very portable as Bland carried away. The lectures form a sort of chronological, though necessarily imperfect, sketch of the whole history of poetry, from that of the Bible down to the songs of Burns. The scheme was magnificent, but it was too vast for one man, especially for a man of Campbell's flighty humour, and he broke away from it before he had well begun. What he has to say about Hebrew and Greek verse is of some value, but generally speaking the thought and the criticism are quite commonplace. Madame de Staël, it is true, told Campbell that, with the exception of Burke's writings there was nothing in English so striking as these lectures. But then it was Madame de Staël who solemnly declared that she had read a certain part of 'The Pleasures of Hope' twenty times, and always with the pleasure of the first reading! She must have known how well praise agreed with the poet. A second course of lectures was delivered at the same institution in 1813, but of these it is not necessary to say more than that, in the conventional language of the day, they were 'applauded to the echo.'

Towards the close of 1813 Campbell's health got 'sadly crazy' again, and he went to Brighton for sea bathing. There he soon found his lost appetite: the fish, he wrote, was delicious, and the library quite a pleasant lounge with the added luxury of music. He called upon Disraeli, 'a good modest man,' and was invited to dine with him. He was also introduced to the venerable Herschel and his son, the one 'a great, simple, good old man,' the other 'a prodigy in science and fond of poetry, but very unassuming.' The astronomer seemed to him like 'a supernatural intelligence,' and when he parted with him he felt 'elevated and overcome.' In such lofty language does Campbell intimate his very simple pleasures and experiences.

But the Brighton holiday was only the prelude to one much longer and much more interesting. During the short-lived peace of 1802 Campbell had often expressed a wish to visit the scenes of the Revolution and above all the Louvre; and now that the abdication of Buonaparte, the capture of Paris, and the presence of the allied armies had drawn thousands of English subjects to the French capital, he resolved to carry out the long-cherished plan. On the 26th of August 1814, he was writing from Dieppe, where one of the rabble called after him: 'Va-t'-en Anglais! vous cherchez nous faire perir de faim.' On the way to Paris he halted for two days at Rouen, where he found his brother Daniel—'poor as ever'—with whom he had parted at Hamburg in 1800. Landing in Paris, he met Mrs Siddons, and in her company visited the Louvre and the Elysian Fields, which he held to be as contemptible in comparison to Hyde Park and the Green Park as the French public squares and buildings are superior to those of London.

At the Louvre, where he spent four hours daily, he grandiloquently says he was struck dumb with emotion, his heart palpitated, and his eyes filled with tears at the sight of that 'immortal youth,' the Belvidere Apollo. Next to the Louvre in interest, he mentions the Jardin des Plantes, 'a sight worth travelling to see.' The Pantheon he describes as 'a magnificent place,' adding that the vaults of Voltaire and Rousseau are the only cleanly things he has seen in Paris; so neat and tidy that they remind him rather of a comfortable English pantry than of anything of an awe-inspiring nature. Versailles is 'very splendid indeed,' but the palace is 'not large enough for the basis, and the trees are clipped with horrible formality.' He is not lost in admiration of the French women. 'There are two sorts of them—the aquiline, or rather nut-cracker faces, and the broad faces; both are ugly.' On the other hand, he finds that the handsomest Englishmen are inferior to the really handsome Frenchmen. The Englishman always looks very John Bullish; and nothing that the French say flatters him so much as when they declare that they would not take him for un Anglois. The Opera he describes as 'a set of silly things, but with some exquisite music'; the French acting in tragedy he does not relish, but their comic acting is perfection. Of notable people whom he met he mentions the elder Schlegel, Humboldt, Cuvier, Denon the Egyptian traveller—'a very pleasing person'—and the Duke of Wellington. To the latter he was introduced merely as 'Mr Campbell,' and the Duke afterwards told Madame de Staël that he 'thought it was one of the thousands of that name from the same country; he did not know it was *the* Thomas.' Schlegel he describes as a very uncommon man, learned and ingenious, but a visionary and a mystic. He and Humboldt, 'after much entreaty,' made him repeat 'Lochiel.' When Schlegel came to England, he was generally Campbell's guest, and the two, notwithstanding that their characters and tastes were so dissimilar, appear to have entertained a sincere regard for each other.

After a two months' stay in Paris, Campbell returned to England, with, as Beattie pompously phrases it, a rich and varied fund of materials for reflection. He found his work much in arrear, and had just begun to make some headway with it when the unlooked-for intelligence reached him that by the death of his Highland cousin, MacArthur Stewart of Ascog, he had fallen heir to a legacy of nearly £5000. The will described him as 'author of "The Pleasures of Hope"'; but it was not for the honours of authorship that he was rewarded. 'Little Tommy, the poet,' said the testator, 'ought to have a legacy because he was so kind as to give his mother sixty pounds yearly out of his income.'

Stewart died at the end of March 1815, and by the middle of April Campbell was in Edinburgh—whither he had gone to look after his interests—feeling 'as blythe as if the devil were dead.' After seeing his old friends in the capital, he went to Kinniel on a visit to Dugald Stewart, and then, taking the Canal boat from Falkirk, set out for Glasgow, where he made a round of his relations. He spent a very happy time altogether, and when he returned to Sydenham, it was, as he thought, to look out on a future of prosperity and comparative ease. A few days after his arrival, Waterloo decided the fate of Europe, and for a time he did nothing but speak and write of the prodigies of British valour performed on that field. Some tributary stanzas written to the tune of 'The British Grenadiers' show that while he did not fancy being taken for an Englishman in Paris, he was very proud to appear as a John Bull jingo at home.

Under his improved prospects he seems to have had some difficulty in settling down to his old literary tasks. We hear of him working again at the eternal 'Specimens,' but otherwise his pen seems to have lain idle. The American heir was coming over in August to take possession of the Ascog estates; and Campbell hoped to reap some additional pecuniary advantages for himself and his sisters. The heir was a cousin of the poet and a brother of the Attorney-General for Virginia. Beattie suggests that if Campbell's elder brother had been aware of the law which rendered aliens to the Crown of Great Britain incapable of inheriting entailed property, and had made up his title as the nearest heir, he might have been proprietor of the old estates, which were afterwards sold for £78,000. But no such luck was to befall the Campbell family. The heir came into possession, and neither Campbell nor his sisters benefited further by his stroke of fortune. Campbell reported that he was an amiable gentleman, but, so far as he could see, was not inclined to be generous. Very likely he considered that Campbell had been well provided for already. At any rate the poet had to content himself, as he might well do, with his pension and his legacy and continue his literary cobbling as before.

His interests now became somewhat more varied. His surviving son had been sent to school, but having had to be removed on account of his health, Campbell set to teach the boy himself. He got up at six every morning and by seven was hammering Greek and Latin into the youth's head. It was all nonsense, he declared, but in his son's interests he dared not act up to his theory, which was to leave Greek and Latin, and instruct him in 'other things.' In Campbell's view it was a vestige of barbarism that 'learning' only means, in its common acceptation, a knowledge of the dead languages and mathematics. Later on he speaks of his intention to drill the lad in 'epistolary habits,' but this intention he was, alas! never able to realise.

While the Greek and Latin lessons were going on, some of Campbell's friends were busy with plans for his benefit. Scott, avowedly anxious to have his personal society, proposed that he should allow himself to be engineered—it was a delicate matter of supplanting an inefficient professor—into the Rhetoric Chair in Edinburgh University. The post was a tempting one, worth from £400 to £500 a year; but nothing is left to show how Campbell took the suggestion. In 1834 he was again urged to appear as a candidate for an Edinburgh professorship, but declined because he expected to live only ten years longer, and it would take him half that time to prepare his lectures. It is not unlikely that he would have regarded the present proposal with favour, but his thoughts were immediately turned in a different direction by the disinterested action of another friend. The Royal Institution had just been opened in Liverpool, and Roscoe was anxious that Campbell should give a dozen lectures there. Some preliminary hitch occurred about the fee, but this was got over, and Campbell ultimately drew no less a sum than £340 from the course. Considering that the lectures were practically those already delivered at the Royal Institution of London, he might compliment himself on being remarkably well paid; yet it is said that when he was afterwards pressed to deliver a second course at Liverpool, presumably on the same terms, he declined.

Campbell made his appearance in Liverpool at the end of October 1818. The lecture-room, wrote one of the listeners some thirty years later, was 'crowded by the *élite* of the neighbourhood.' The lecturer's prose 'was declared to be more poetic than his poetry; his glowing imagination gave a double charm to those passages from the poets which he cited as illustrations. The effect and animation of his eye, his figure, his voice, in reciting these passages are still vividly remembered.' From Liverpool he went on to Birmingham, where he received £100 for repeating the lectures there. At Birmingham 'it pleased fate that Thomas should take the measles,' and Campbell himself had to get blisters applied to his chest to relieve his breathing. Under the circumstances he could not be expected to visit much; but he was introduced to Miss Edgeworth, who captivated him by the unassuming simplicity of her manner, and he 'met L—d [Lloyd], the quondam partner of L—b [Lamb] in poetry— an innocent creature, but imagines everybody dead.' He called upon Gregory Watt's father—*the* James Watt—with whom, though he was then eighty-three, he says he spent one of the most amusing days he ever had with a man of science and a stranger to his own pursuits.

Suggestions had reached him from Glasgow and Edinburgh that he should deliver his lectures in these towns, but although, with his usual facility, he had come to think that lecturing was likely to be his *metier*, at present he literally had not a voice to exert without imminent hazard. And there was another danger. 'I know well,' he says, 'what would happen from the hospitality of Glasgow or Edinburgh… I should enjoy the hospitality to the prejudice of my health. For though I now abstain habitually from even the ordinary indulgence in eating and taking wine, yet the excitement of speaking always hurts me.' And so, partly to avoid the conviviality which Dickens and Thackeray enjoyed later as lecturers in Edinburgh and Glasgow, Campbell declined the invitations from the north, and went home to Sydenham.

While he was absent on this literary tour, the long-delayed 'Specimens of the British Poets'—Miss Mitford makes very merry over the time spent on the work—had at length been published in seven octavo volumes. It proved only a moderate success. The plan was well conceived, but Campbell committed the initial mistake of deciding to print, not the best specimens of his authors, but only such pieces mainly as had not been printed by Ellis and by Headley. Of Sir Philip Sidney, for example, he says: 'Mr Ellis has exhausted the best specimens of his poetry; I have only offered a few short ones.' The absurdity of this procedure need not be pointed out. People do not go to a book of specimens for examples of a writer in his second-best manner. They want the cream of a poet, not, as Campbell has too often given them, the skimmed milk of his genius.

But the work was faulty on other grounds. Its biographical and bibliographical information was notoriously incorrect and imperfect. Campbell had no taste for the drudgery of antiquarian research: not in his line, he boldly announced, was the labour of trying to discover the number of Milton's house in Bunhill Fields. His facts as a natural consequence were never to be depended upon. In the 'Specimens' the inaccuracies are more than usually abundant, and would, even if the work were otherwise satisfactory, entirely discount its value. 'Read Campbell's Poets,' said Byron in his Journal; 'marked the errors of Tom for correction.' Again: 'Came home—read. Corrected Tom Campbell's slips of the pen.' Some of Tom's errors were, no doubt, mere slips; but more were clearly attributable to ignorance and laziness. If, for example, he had been at the trouble to take his Shakespeare from the shelf he would never have been guilty of such a misquotation as the following:

To gild refined gold, to paint the *lily*,

To throw a perfume on the violet.

The work absolutely bristles with errors of this kind. Of the introductory essay and the prefatory notices of the various writers it is possible to speak somewhat more favourably. The essay, though written in an affected style, is still worth reading, especially the portions dealing with Milton and Pope. The lives, again, are marked by a fair appreciation of the powers of the respective poets, from the point of view of the old school; and although there is nothing subtle in the criticisms, there is welcome evidence of that sympathetic spirit which loves poetry for its own sake. This is the most that can be said for a work which Lockhart unaccountably eulogised as 'not unworthy to be handed down with the classical verse of its author.' No second edition of it was called for before 1841, when Campbell had some difference with Murray about its revision. Murray's original agreement with Campbell had been for £500, but when the work was completed he doubled that sum and added books to the value of £200 which Campbell had borrowed. This munificent generosity Campbell rewarded by refusing to correct his own errors, though he was offered a handsome sum to do so; and the result was that he had to submit to the 'Specimens' being silently revised by another hand. The incident, which is not a little damaging to Campbell's character, proves again that Campbell was treated by the booksellers far more liberally than he deserved.

Having disposed of the 'Specimens,' he was free to look about for other work. At the beginning of 1820 he tells a friend that he has a new poem on the anvil, with several small ones lying by, and only waits until he has enough for a volume to publish them. He is to lecture again at the Royal Institution in the Spring, and as both his fellow-lecturers have been knighted, he thinks it not unlikely that he will be knighted too. On the whole he was in excellent spirits; and the necessity for unremitting toil having been removed, he began to arrange for a holiday. This time he decided to revisit Germany, and having let his house furnished for a year, and concluded his lecture course, he embarked with his family for Holland in the end of May.

Landing at Rotterdam, with the view of which from the Maas he was 'much captivated,' he proceeded by the Hague and Leyden to Haarlem, where he was 'transported' with the famous organ in the Cathedral. From Amsterdam he wrote to say that the faces of the people were as unromantic as the face of their country, but he was pleased to see their houses 'so painted and cleaned' that poverty could have no possible terrors for them. At Bonn he renewed his acquaintance with Schlegel, who on this occasion bored him sadly. Schlegel, it seems, was ludicrously fond of showing off his English. He thought he understood English politics, too, and pestered Campbell with his crude speculations about England's impending bankruptcy and the misery of her lower orders. 'I had no notion,' says Campbell, 'that a great man could ever grow so wearisome.'

Leaving his son, now in his sixteenth year, with Professor Kapp, who was to board and instruct him for £5 a month, he went to Frankfort, visiting on the way the Rolandseck, where he wrote his 'Roland the Brave.' At Frankfort he had daily lessons in German from a Carthusian monk, who was rather surprised at his strange plan of overcoming the difficulties of the language by dint of Greek. At Ratisbon he revived many memories. Of the twelve monks whom he had known at the Scots College in 1800, only two were now alive; but their successors were 'very liberal of their beer, and it is by no means contemptible.' When he got to Vienna—where he read Hebrew with a Jewish poet named Cohen—he found that his fame had preceded him. His arrival was publicly announced, translations of 'Ye Mariners' and the Kirnan 'Lines' appeared in one of the leading journals, and invitations showered in upon him from the best people in the capital. He met a large number of the Polish nobility, who crowded about him with affectionate zeal. He forgot all his sorrows listening to the organ in St Stephen's. The theatres he found tiresome. The actors indeed were good, but what could they make of such a language? From Vienna he returned to Bonn through Bavaria. He was now impatient to be home; and, having transferred his son to the care of Dr Meyer, he bade farewell to his friends, and was in London by the end of November.

Before leaving for the Continent he had entered into an agreement with Colburn for editing the *New Monthly Magazine* for three years, from January 1821. He was to have £500 per annum, and was to furnish annually six contributions in prose and six in verse. Campbell had not shown any special fitness for the duties of an editor, but he knew the value of his own name, which, indeed, was probably the reason of Colburn's applying to him. He had, as Patmore says, the most extensive and the most unquestioned reputation of the writers of the day, and the proprietor's judgment was soon proved by the unprecedented popularity of the magazine. Campbell certainly showed some zeal at the start. He got together a very efficient staff of contributors, with Mr Cyrus Redding as his sub-editor. Moreover, in order to be near the office he decided to exchange his Sydenham house for one in town, and he took private lodgings in Margaret Street until a permanent residence could be found. There, shutting himself up from outside society, he 'received and consulted with his friends, cultivated acquaintance with literary men of all parties, answered correspondents, pretended to read contributions, wrote new and revised old papers, and, in short, identified his own reputation and interests with those of the magazine.' The *New Monthly*, for the time being, became the record of his literary life.

With all this show of work, Campbell, by every account, proved a very unsatisfactory editor, though no more unsatisfactory than Bulwer Lytton and Theodore Hook who succeeded him. Allowing for the probable exaggeration of his own importance as sub-editor, there is enough in Redding's reminiscences to show that he found his position difficult enough. Campbell had so little acquaintance with periodical literature that he declares he never saw a number of the *New Monthly* until Colburn put one into his hands! He gave no attention to the topics of the day, and his knowledge of current literature was so limited that contributors often foisted on him articles which they had furtively abstracted from contemporary writers. Of method he had none. His papers lay about in hopeless confusion, and if he wanted to get rid of them for the time, he would jumble them into a heap, or cram them into a drawer. Articles sent by contributors would be placed over his books on the shelves, slip down behind and lie forgotten. He always shied at the perusal of manuscripts, and he kept the printer continually waiting for 'copy.' Talfourd says he would balance contending epithets for a fortnight, and stop the press for a week to determine the value of a comma. In short, he was the very worst imaginable kind of editor, especially from the contributor's point of view. Nevertheless, he soon drew a strong brigade of writers around him—among them Hazlitt, Talfourd, Horace Smith, and Henry Roscoe—and placing implicit confidence in their work, he made his editorship a snug sinecure. 'Tom Campbell,' said Scott, 'had much in his power. A man at the head of a magazine may do much for young men, but Campbell did nothing, more from indolence, I fancy, than disinclination or a bad heart.' That was the true word; Campbell, to use the expressive term of his countrymen, simply could not be 'fashed.'

While things were proceeding thus in the editorial sanctum a painful crisis was approaching in Campbell's domestic affairs. He had not long returned from the Continent when reports of his son began to give him uneasiness. Thomas, he says, talks of going to sea, which indicates that he is not disposed to do much good on land. Early in the spring of 1821 the youth turned up in London. He had been transferred from Bonn to Amiens, but disliking the place and the people, he had run away from his instructor. Campbell was greatly affected by his unexpected arrival, but Tony M'Cann, who was in the house, proposed to celebrate the event by killing the fatted calf! In the autumn the boy was sent to a school at Poplar, at a cost to his father of £120 per annum, but he had not been many weeks there when symptoms, the meaning of which had hitherto been mistaken, became so pronounced that he had to be removed to an asylum. It is a distressing subject, and there is no need to go into details. Young Campbell was ultimately placed under the care of Dr Matthew Allen at High Beech, Essex. There he chiefly remained until three months after his father's death in 1844, when he was liberated by the verdict of a jury declaring him to be of sound mind. The taint of insanity clearly came from the mother's side. One of her sisters had been deranged for many years before her death; and indeed it has been hinted that Mrs Campbell herself suffered from some 'mental alienation' during her last days. A writer in Hogg's *Weekly Instructor* for April 12, 1845, expressly says so. He seems to have known Campbell, but his statement, so far as can be ascertained, is uncorroborated.

In 1822 Campbell removed to a small house of his own at 10 West Seymour Street—a 'beautiful creation,' with 'the most amiable curtains, the sweetest of carpets, the most accomplished chairs, and a highly interesting set of tongs and fenders.' Here he wrote one of his best things and one of his worst. 'The Last Man' was published in the *New Monthly* in 1823. Gilfillan calls it the most Christian of all Campbell's strains. It is, in fact, one of the most striking of his shorter productions. The same idea was used by Byron in his 'Darkness,' and this led to some controversy as to which of the two poets had been guilty of stealing from the other. Campbell maintained that he had many years before mentioned to Byron his intention of writing the poem, and there is no reason to doubt his word. Of course the idea of one man, the last of his race, remaining when all else has been destroyed, is quite an obvious one; and in any case Campbell treated it in a manner altogether different from Byron, of whose daring misanthropy he was completely innocent.

It has been said that at West Seymour Street Campbell also wrote one of his worst poems. This was his 'Theodric,' not 'Theodoric,' as it is constantly mis-spelled. He seems to have been engaged on it early in 1823; but he confesses that so far from being in a poetic mood he is barely competent for the dull duty of editorship. It is well to remember this in judging the poem. He had begun it at a time when horrible dreams of his son being tortured by asylum attendants disturbed his rest; he had finished it with the obstreperous youth temporarily at home—outrageous, dogged, and disagreeable, 'excessively anxious to convince us how very cordially he hates both his mother and me.' He knew that 'Theodric' had faults, but he regarded these as so little detrimental that he believed when it recovered from the first buzz of criticism it would attain a steady popularity. It appeared in November 1824, but the popularity which Campbell anticipated never came to it. 'I am very glad,' he says, 'that Jeffrey is going to review me, for I think *he* has the stuff in him to understand "Theodric."' But neither Jeffrey nor anybody else understood 'Theodric'; certainly nobody appreciated it. The wits at Holland House disowned it; the *Quarterly* called it 'an unworthy publication'; and friend joined foe in the chorus of condemnation. An anonymous punster referred to it as the 'odd trick' of the season; and its excessively overdone alliterations (such as 'Heights browsed by the bounding bouquetin') were made the subject of scornful hilarity. The poem, in truth, was a sad failure, and the universal censure with which it met was thoroughly deserved. Campbell had 'attempted to imitate the natural simplicity and homely familiarity of the style of Crabbe and Wordsworth,' and had only succeeded in becoming elaborately tame and feeble.

Just before the publication of 'Theodric,' he had paid a short visit to Cheltenham for his health's sake; now he went to Lord Spencer's at Althorp, 'a most beautiful Castle of Indolence,' tempted by the hope of seeing books which he could not see elsewhere. He really wanted to study, yet he capriciously complained that after breakfast the company, including his Lordship, went off to shoot and left him alone! In short, he was no sooner at Althorp than he wished himself home again.

When he returned to town, in January 1825, it was to take part in what he afterwards called the only important event in his career. This was the founding of the London University, the idea of which he appears to have conceived during his recent intercourse with the Professors of Bonn. The scheme was discussed at various private and public conferences during the spring and summer, and the financial basis of the undertaking being apparently assured, Campbell proceeded to Berlin in September to ascertain how far the University there might serve as a model for London. He spent a week in the Prussian capital, which he compares unfavourably with London in everything but cookery, and came away with 'every piece of information respecting the University,' and every book he wished for. At Hamburg he was given a public dinner by eighty English residents, and was driven about the town by his old *protégé*, the 'Exile of Erin.' Back in London, he appeared at a meeting in support of the Western Literary and Scientific Institution, and in an eloquent speech declared that if his plan of a Metropolitan University succeeded he would ask for no other epitaph on his grave than to be celebrated as one of its originators. The plan, fortunately, did succeed, and although Lord Brougham, to serve his own political ambitions, tried to rob him of the honour, there cannot be a doubt that it rightly belongs to Campbell. Moreover, King's College would never have existed but for the London University, so that Campbell, as he used to remark, did a double good.

Meanwhile, at the beginning of 1826, he was interesting himself in certain domestic affairs. He was having a spacious study constructed, and he proposed to treat himself to a new carpet and some elegant leather chairs. Every volume was to be removed from the drawing-room; and henceforth he was to smoke in a garret, not in his study. His fancy also rioted by anticipation in 'a geranium-coloured paper with gold leaves to harmonise with the glory of my gilded and red-bound books.' But there his purse and his vanity were at loggerheads. While the masons were hammering in the house, the Glasgow students had decided to ask Campbell to allow himself to be put forward as their Lord Rector. At first he complied, but as the time approached he began to waver in his decision. He was not well, his son's malady distressed him, and his pecuniary affairs—thanks in a great measure to his own reckless extravagance—were again in deep water. Writing on November 6 (1826) he says: 'I got in bills on Saturday morning for the making up of my new house, treble the amount expected; and also confirmation of an acquaintance being bankrupt, for whom I had advanced the deposits on three shares in the London University. I could not now accept the Rectorship if it were at my option. If I travelled it must be on borrowed money. Friends I have in plenty who would lend, but I fear debt as I do the bitterness of death.' This seemed decisive enough, and yet nine days later the Principal of Glasgow University was announcing to him that he had been elected Lord Rector by the unanimous vote of the four 'nations.'

The rival candidates were Mr Canning and Sir Thomas Brisbane, and the contest had proved more than usually exciting, from the fact that all the professors except Millar and Jardine were opposed to Campbell on the not very solid ground of 'political distrust.' Some enemy even sought to damage his cause by circulating a report that his mother had been 'a washerwoman in the Goosedubs of Glasgow.' Wilson, referring in the 'Noctes Ambrosianæ' to this incident, remarked that in England such baseness would be held incredible; but Wilson forgot that the fight was practically a political one, and in politics any stick is, or was, good enough to beat a dog with. Campbell's triumph was, however, all the greater that it was achieved under such conditions; and we can easily imagine the glow of pride with which he went down to Glasgow in the succeeding April (1827).

He landed on the 9th of the month, after a journey which he had cause to remember from the circumstance that Matilda brought 'seventy parcels of baggage,' and on the 12th he delivered his inaugural address in the old College Hall. There is abundant evidence of his high spirits in an incident recorded by Allan Cunningham. Snow lay on the ground at the time, and when Campbell reached the College Green he found the students pelting each other. 'The poet ran into the ranks, threw several snowballs with unerring aim, then, summoning the scholars around him in the Hall, delivered a speech replete with philosophy and eloquence.' The snowballing was not very dignified perhaps, but it was strictly in character, and must have added immensely to Campbell's popularity with the 'darling boys' of his Alma Mater. The Rectorial address was received with intense enthusiasm. One listener describes it as elegant and highly poetical, and says that it was delivered with great ease and dignity. Another, a student, writes: 'To say we applauded is to say nothing. We evinced every symptom of respect and admiration, from the loftiest tribute, even our tears—drawn forth by his eloquent recollections of olden times—down to escorting him with boisterous noise along the public streets.'

Campbell remained in Glasgow until the 1st of May, banqueting with the Professors and the Senatus (who, by the way, created him an LL.D., a title which he never used), hearing explanations by the Faculty, and coaching himself up in University ordinances and finance. For Campbell filled the Rectorial office in no sinecure fashion. Perhaps, as Redding says, he made more of the post than it was worth, out of a little harmless vanity and somewhat of local attachment. But at any rate he did not spare himself. He got his inaugural address printed, and sent every student a copy of it, inscribed with his autograph. He wrote a series of Letters on the Epochs of Greek and Roman Literature, which, after running through the *New Monthly*, he presented to the students in volume form. He investigated the rights of the students too, and secured them many advantages of which they had been unjustly deprived. All these duties he performed in person, thus involving several special journeys to Glasgow; so that, on the whole, it may safely be said that he conducted himself like a model Lord Rector.

The result was seen in his re-election, not only for a second but for a third term, which was almost unprecedented, and indeed was said to be contrary to the statutes and usage of the University. His popularity with the students all through was very great. They founded a Campbell Club in his honour; commissioned a full-length portrait by Sir Thomas Lawrence; and presented him with a silver punch-bowl, which figures in his will as one of his 'jewels.' When he was elected for the third time they went wild with delight. Campbell was staying with his cousin, Mr Gray, in Great Clyde Street, a few paces from the river. There the students gathered to the number of fourteen hundred, and a speech being called for, Campbell appeared at the window. 'Students,' he said, 'sooner shall that river'—pointing to the Clyde—'cease to flow into the sea, than I, while I live, will forget the honour this day done to me.' There is but one step from the sublime to the ridiculous. At this stage an old washerwoman passing on the outskirts of the crowd was arrested by the sight of what she conceived to be a lunatic speaking from a window. 'Puir man!' she remarked to a student, 'can his freends no tak' him in?' A royal time it must have been for the poet in Glasgow altogether. He was naturally much attached to the city, and although he complains of feeling melancholy while walking about his old haunts, yet it was a melancholy not without alleviations. The Rectorship had been 'a sunburst of popular favour,' the 'crowning honour' of his life; and as for Glasgow itself, why it flowed with 'syllogisms and ale.'

The third year of Campbell's Rectorship expired in the autumn of 1829, but meanwhile, in May 1828, he had lost his wife. Mrs Campbell had been ailing for some time, and his anxiety on her account darkens all the correspondence of the period. For several months he acted both as housekeeper and sick-nurse, and seldom crossed his door except to get something for the invalid. Mrs Campbell's death was an irreparable loss to him. She had been an affectionate, even a childishly adoring wife (she used to take visitors upstairs on tiptoe to show the poet 'in a moment of inspiration'!) and it does not surprise us to read of the bereaved husband relieving his feelings with tears at the sight of a trinket or a knot of ribbon that belonged to her. Mrs Campbell had tributes from many quarters. Redding said that no praise could be too high for her good management and her general conduct in domestic life. Mrs Grant of Laggan, writing of Campbell's pecuniary embarrassments, remarked that 'his good, gentle, patient little wife was so frugal, so sweet-tempered, that she might have disarmed poverty of half its evils.' It was maliciously hinted in Scotland that she lived unhappily with her husband, but upon that point we may safely accept the testimony of Redding. 'I never,' he says, 'found Mrs Campbell out of temper. I never saw a remote symptom of disagreement, though I entered the poet's house for years at all times, without ceremony. I believe the tale to be wholly a fiction.'

Mrs Campbell's death sent the poet out into the world and into company very different from that with which he had been used to associate. Redding makes touching reference to the change at his fireside. The recollection of Mrs Campbell's uniform cheerfulness and hospitality, the sight of her tea-table without her presence, her vacant chair, that inexpressible lack of something which long custom had made like second nature—these things gave to Campbell's home a melancholy colouring which his old friends never cared to contemplate. 'Man,' says Lytton, 'may have a splendid palace, a comfortable lodging, nay, even a pleasant house, but man has no home where the home has no mistress.' Henceforward Campbell had practically no home. He moved about from house to house, always seeking the comfort which he never found, his books and his papers and his general belongings getting ever into a greater state of confusion for want of the hand that had so quietly and skilfully ordered his domestic affairs.

The literary product of these years of bereavement and the Glasgow Rectorship was naturally very slight. Indeed the letters to the students, already mentioned, formed almost the only writings of any importance. In concert with the elder students he projected a Classical Encyclopædia, but for some unexplained reason the project was allowed to drop. The victory of Navarino in October 1827 produced some stanzas which he not inaptly called 'a rumble-tumble concern,' and the 'Lines to Julia M——,' as well as the short lyric, 'When Love came first to Earth,' seem to have been written in 1829. It was, however, an essentially barren period, unmarked by a single piece above the average of the third-rate writer.

CHAPTER VIII
CLOSING YEARS

Some time just before the expiration of his Rectorship at Glasgow in 1829, Campbell changed his residence from Seymour Street to Middle Scotland Yard, where he furnished on such a grand scale that he had to mortgage a prospective edition of his poems to pay the bill. In connection with this change there were hints of a second marriage—hints which continued to be whispered about for many a day, to Campbell's evident annoyance. He declared that there was no foundation for the report, that it was 'the baseless fabric of a vision'; yet we are assured by Beattie that he took his new house at the suggestion of 'an amiable and accomplished friend deeply interested in his welfare, and destined, as he fondly imagined, to restore him to the happiness of married life.' Who the amiable lady was we are not told; nor is anything said as to why the engagement fell through. The presumption is that Campbell changed his mind, and did not want to have the matter discussed.

At this time a suitable marriage would certainly have been no act of madness, for Campbell was clearly feeling himself more than usually lonesome. Indeed, it was with the avowed object of mitigating his forlorn condition that he established the Literary Union, a social club over which he presided till he finally left London in 1843. The burden of work and removal had again thrown him into a wretched state of health, and in September (1829) he writes to say that he is doing next to nothing apart from the *New Monthly*. Protracted study exhausts him, and he dare not take wine, which is the only reviving stimulus left. Starvation alone alleviates his distress: a hearty meal means an agony of suffering; therefore he stints himself at table, and loses flesh daily.

So the beginning of 1830 found him. His friend Sir Thomas Lawrence had just died, and although he was profoundly ignorant of the technique of art, and had even a limited appreciation of pictures and painting, he boldly undertook to write the artist's life. He set to the work in a comically serious fashion. He had a printed notice sent to his friends and fastened to the door of his study, intimating his desire to be left undisturbed till the book was finished. These notices—for Campbell issued them regularly—were the subject of much merriment among his acquaintances. It was an announcement of the kind that drew from Hook the jest about Campbell having been safely delivered of a couplet. In the present case the ruse apparently did not answer, for in a week or two he fled to the country. He seems to have spent a good deal of time over the Life, but nothing ever came of his labours. Colburn insisted on having the book in a few months, and Campbell, declaring that he could 'get no materials,' petulantly threw it aside.

This was in December 1830. By that time Campbell had severed his connection with the *New Monthly*. Colburn had parted with Redding in October, and the editor's difficulties were in consequence greatly increased. He went out of town, and in his absence an attack on his old friend, Dr Glennie of Dulwich, was inadvertently passed by Redding's successor, Mr S. C. Hall. Campbell does not explicitly say that this incident was the cause of his resignation, but as he mentions interminable scrapes and threatened law-suits, we may safely assume that it was. At any rate he said good-bye to Colburn in no amiable mood. Colburn had a bill of £700 against him, partly for books and partly for the expense of the current unsold edition of his poems. How was he to discharge such a debt? The difficulty was temporarily met by an agreement with Cochrane, the publisher, whereby the latter was to pay the £700 in return for Campbell's undertaking the editorship of a new venture, to be called *The Metropolitan Magazine*, and for two hundred unsold copies of his poems in Colburn's hands. Unluckily, Cochrane could not make up the £700, and Campbell, in order to satisfy Colburn, had to stake the rent of his house and sell off his poems at such price as they would bring. At the close of 1830 he went into lodgings, and instead of settling down, as he had hoped, to enjoy a kind of mild *otium cum dignitate*, he had perforce to resume his seat on the thorny cushion of the editorial chair. When he left the *New Monthly*, Redding asked him, 'What about the reduced finances?' 'Devil take the finances,' said he; 'it is something to be free if a man has but a shirt and a carpet bag.' His soreness of heart at having to sell his liberty again may thus be imagined.

Campbell's connection with the *Metropolitan Magazine* proved anything but agreeable. True, things went smoothly enough for a time. In the autumn he felt himself ten inches taller because he had got a third share in the property. The share cost him £500, and he had to borrow the money from Rogers, for whose security—though Rogers generously declined any security—he insured his life and pledged his library and house furniture. But the concern turned out to be a bubble, and Campbell suffered agonies of suspense about his money. He got it back in the long run, and it was returned to Rogers. But this was only the beginning of his troubles. At the request of Captain Chamier, one of the proprietors, he continued in the editorship, but the magazine passed through many vicissitudes. When it came into the hands of his old friend Captain Marryat, Campbell wanted to cut connection with it entirely, and was prevailed upon to remain only by Marryat promising to relieve him of the correspondence. Shortly after this, Marryat offered the editorship to Moore who, however, declined to supplant Campbell, and so joined the staff merely as a contributor. Campbell presently reported that 'we go on in very good heart.' But these conditions did not last. Campbell found that he could not work comfortably under Marryat—who was just about to give the magazine a swing with his 'Peter Simple'—and he threw up the editorship, which in point of fact he had held only in name. He seems to have left everything to his sub-editor. He seldom examined a manuscript unless it came from one of his friends; nor did he give by his contributions—nine short pieces of verse—anything like value for the money he received. His editorship, in short, was purely ornamental.

But it is necessary to retrace our steps. Just after taking on the *Metropolitan* in 1831, Campbell fixed upon a quiet residence at St Leonard's which he now used as an occasional retreat from the bustle of London. We hear of him strolling with complacent pride on the beach while the band played 'The Campbells are Comin'' and 'Ye Mariners of England.' He tells his sister that refined female society had become of great consequence to him, and that he found it concentrated here. He had no pressing engagements, and accordingly had written more verses than he had done for many years within the same time. His 'Lines on the View from St Leonards,' published first in the *Metropolitan*, were well-known, though they are now forgotten. A visit to one of the paper mills at Maidstone in July 1831 was made to inquire about the price of paper for an edition of 'The Pleasures of Hope' which Turner had promised to illustrate. Campbell had a little joke with the manager at the mills. 'I am a paper-stainer,' he said, and then he explained that he stained with author's ink, after which the manager became 'intensely disdainful.' At Stoke, near Bakewell, whither he had gone to see Mrs Arkwright, a daughter of Stephen Kemble, he heard Chevalier Neukomm play the organ. This, he says, was as great an era in his sensations as when he first beheld the Belvidere Apollo. In the music he imagined that he heard his dead Alison speaking to him from heaven, and when he could listen no longer he slipped out to the churchyard, where he 'gave way to almost convulsive sensations.' Some years later he met Neukomm again, and at his request turned a part of the Book of Job—the 'sublime text' of which he often extolled—into verse for an oratorio. The effort appears as a 'fragment' in his works, and Neukomm is said to have composed the music, though no mention of such an oratorio is made in any of the biographical notices of the composer.

We come now to an important episode in the life of Campbell—an episode which for long engaged almost his sole attention. His interest in the cause of Poland had already been strikingly expressed in 'The Pleasures of Hope.' It was an interest which, as his friend Dr Madden puts it, had all the strength of a passion, all the fervour of patriotism. Poland was his idol. 'He wrote for it, he worked for it, he sold his literary labour for it; he used his influence with all persons of eminence in political life of his acquaintance in favour of it; and, when it was lost, in favour of those brave defenders of it who had survived its fall. He threw himself heart and soul into the cause; he identified all his feelings, nay, his very being with it.' The names of Czartoryski and Niemeiewitz were never off his lips. A tale of a distressed Pole was his greeting to friends when they met; a subscription the chorus of his song. In fact, he was quite mad on the subject, as mad as ever Byron was about Greece, or Boswell about Corsica.

What roused him first was the fall of Warsaw, by the news of which he was so affected that Madden feared for his life or his reason. He began very practically by subscribing £100 to the Warsaw Hospital Fund, 'a mighty sum for a poor poet,' as he says in an unpublished letter. He had written some 'Lines on Poland' for the *Metropolitan*, and these, along with the Lines on St Leonards, he proposed to publish in a *brochure*, by which he expected to raise £50 more. The number of exiles in London gradually increased. Many of them were starving. Campbell constituted himself their guardian, appealed urgently for money on their behalf, and subsequently, early in 1831, founded a Polish Association with the object of relieving distress and distributing literature calculated to arouse public sympathy on the matter.

Of this Association he was appointed chairman. The duties proved anything but light. In June 1832 he writes that he has a heavy correspondence to keep up, both with friends at home and with foreigners. He has letters in French, German, and even Latin to write, and these afford him nothing like a sinecure. There was also a monthly journal called *Polonia* to edit; besides which the German question—another and the same with the Polish— involved him in much vexatious correspondence with the patriots of the Fatherland. At this date he was constantly working from seven in the morning till midnight; he even changed his dinner hour to two o'clock to have a longer afternoon for his beloved Poles. It was impossible that such a strain could last; and at length, in May 1833, he withdrew from the Association as having become too arduous and exciting for his health. Thus closed a part of his career which was as honourable to him as anything he ever did, and upon which he looked back with feelings of sad pleasure. His zeal was perhaps a little ill-regulated, but his sincerity and his active practical efforts on behalf of many brave, unfortunate men bore the impress of a noble and a generous nature. The Poles showed their gratitude in many touching ways; and we have his own express declaration that only once in his life did he experience anything at all like their warm-hearted recognition of his services on their behalf.

During the whole of this distracted period Campbell had all but completely forsaken his own proper business. He had, of course, continued to edit the *Metropolitan*, and his random contributions to that journal must have filled up some time, but from the fall of Warsaw in March 1831 to his ceasing connection with the Polish Association in May 1833 his interests were centred entirely on the affairs of the exiles. Even the agitation about the Reform Bill had passed almost unheeded, though he was among those who celebrated the passing of the Bill by dining with the Lord Mayor at the

Guildhall, on which occasion he remarked that the turtle soup tasted as if it had already felt the beneficent effects of Reform. From Glasgow had come in 1832 an appeal that he would allow himself to be nominated as a candidate for Parliament, but he declined the honour because a seat in the House would entail a life of 'dreadful hardship,' and cut up his literary occupation.

The only work of any note which he did while actively interested in the Poles was the Life of Mrs Siddons. He finished the book, at the end of 1832, in one volume, but the 'tyrant booksellers' would not look at it until he had expanded it into two volumes. It was at length published in June 1834. Few words need be wasted over it. Mrs Siddons, of whom he entertained an extravagantly high opinion, had entrusted him with what he loftily termed the 'sacred duty' of writing her life, but he was thoroughly unfitted for such a commission, and it is the simple truth that no man of even average ability ever produced a worse biography. The *Quarterly* called it 'an abuse of biography,' and its author 'the worst theatrical historian we have ever had.' It is full of the grossest blunders, and some of its expressions are turgid and nonsensical beyond belief. Thus of Mrs Pritchard we read that she 'electrified the house with disappointment,' a statement upon which the *Quarterly* remarked: 'This, we suppose, is what the philosophers call negative electricity.' The thing was rendered additionally absurd by the noise which Campbell had made about the writing of the book. He talked about it and wrote about it to everybody, as if it were to be the *magnum opus* of his life. From this the public and his friends naturally formed great expectations, and when they found they had been deluded they covered Campbell with ridicule.

With the money which the publication of this wretched book brought him Campbell now afforded himself a long break. He conceived the idea of a classical pilgrimage in Italy as likely not only to benefit his health but to furnish him with materials for a new poem. A change in the tide of his affairs carried him however to Paris, and he never set eyes on the sunny land. He arrived in the French capital in July, when the weather was so hot that he told the Parisians their *beau climat* was fit only for devils. He was eagerly welcomed by many of the Polish exiles, who gave him, what he did not dislike, a grand dinner, at which Prince Czartoryski proclaimed him 'the pleader, the champion, the zealous and unwearied apostle of our holy cause.' He heard Louis Philippe deliver his address to the Peers and Deputies, and made a 'dispassionate enquiry' into the characteristics of French beauty, which resulted in the conviction that the French ladies have no beauty at all! He began work on a Geography of Classical History, rising every morning with the sun, and studying for twelve hours a day. Presently some French friends interested him in the recent conquest and colonisation of Algiers, and, with his characteristic caprice, he decided to go there at once and write a book on the colony.

He landed in Algiers on the 18th of September (1834) to find Captain St Palais translating his poems for publication. 'Prancing gloriously' on an Arabian barb, he felt as if he had dropt into a new planet. The vegetation gave him ecstatic delight, and he was greatly elated when he discovered some ruins unmentioned by previous travellers. As usual he began to harass himself about money, but the announcement opportunely arrived that Telford had left him £1000, and he resolved to go on with his tour. He covered the entire coast from Bona to Oran, and penetrated as far as Mascara, seventy miles into the interior. For several nights he slept under the tents of the Arabs, and he made much of hearing a lion roar in his 'native savage freedom.' But all this, and a great deal more, may be read in his 'Letters from the South,' an informative and even lively work in two volumes, which appeared originally in the *New Monthly*. Campbell's account of Algerian scenery is so glowingly eloquent that if unforeseen objects had not diverted his attention, the African tour would probably have formed the subject of a new poem. As it was, the tour remained poetically barren, save for some lines on a dead eagle and a *jeu d'esprit* written for the British Consul's children.

Campbell was back in Paris in May 1835, and after 'a long and gracious audience' with Louis Philippe, he returned to London to tell more stories than Tom Coryatt, and enjoy a temporary fame as an African traveller. The tour seems, however, to have done him harm rather than good. Redding says he was astonished at the change in his appearance. He looked a dozen years older; he was in unusually low spirits, and he kept harping upon his disordered constitution. From this date onwards the record of his career is not worth dwelling upon in any detail. He suffered greatly from spells of ill-health; he shifted fitfully from one residence to another; he visited this place and that place; and with constant cackle about his busy pen, did almost nothing. Under these circumstances the briefest summary of the remaining years of his life will suffice.

Upon his return from Paris in 1835 he settled down at York Chambers, St James' Street, where he prepared his 'Letters from the South' and arranged about the new edition of his poems to be illustrated by Turner. In May 1836 he started for Scotland, where he remained for four months, spending, he says, the happiest time he had ever spent in the land of his fathers. On former visits he had always been hurried and haunted by the necessity of sending manuscripts or proofs to London; but now he was his own master. At Glasgow he dined with the Campbell Club, and got over the function 'very well,' having left Professor Wilson and other choice spirits to prolong the carousal into the small hours. *Apropos*, a story is told of Wilson and Campbell which is too good to be missed. The poet's cousin, Mr Gray, had a bewitchingly pretty maid, who had set Campbell—so he says—dreaming about the heroines of romance. The day after the dinner, Wilson, with other members of the Club, called at the house while the Gray family were absent. 'I rang to get refreshment for them,' says Campbell, 'and fair Margaret brought it in. The Professor looked at her with so much admiration that I told him in Latin to contain his raptures, and he did so; but rose and walked round the room like a lion pacing his cage. Before parting he said, "Cawmel, that might be your ain Gertrude. Could not you just ring and get me a sight of that vision of beauty again?" "No, no," I told him, "get you gone, you Moral Philosophy loon, and give my best respects to your wife and daughters."' As a set-off to this, it may be recorded that Campbell was sadly dismayed at seeing so many of the Glasgow 'bonnie lassies' going about with bare feet. 'I am constantly,' he says, 'preaching against this national disgrace to my countrymen. It is a barbarism so unlike, so unworthy of, the otherwise civilised character of the commonality, which is the most intelligent in Europe; and it is a disgrace unpalliated by poverty in Glasgow, where the industrious are exceedingly well-off.' The Club dinner was followed by a meeting of the Polish Association, at which Campbell gave a forty-five minutes' speech that, by his own report, caused quite a sensation. He went to hear his old College chum, Dr Wardlaw, preach, and afterwards compared him with Chalmers. Chalmers, he said, 'carries his audience by storm, but Wardlaw is a reasoning and well-informed person,' a double-edged compliment to the more famous divine which Campbell probably did not see.

After a trip to the Highlands—one result of which was his 'Lines to Ben Lomond,' published shortly after in the *Scenic Annual*—he went to Edinburgh, where, on the 5th of August, he was made a freeman and was fêted like a prince. The Paisley Council and bailies, as he humorously tells, refused him a like honour; they bestowed it on Wilson, who was an inveterate Tory, and denied it to Campbell because he was a Whig. Nevertheless, Campbell, taking no offence, went to Paisley to the dinner, and Wilson and he spent a merry time at the races afterwards, Campbell being, indeed, so 'prodigiously interested' as to have an even £50 on one of the events!

Returning to London in October, he was back in Scotland again in the summer of 1837. There was a printers' centenary festival in the capital in July, and nobody could be got to take the chair 'because it was a three-and-sixpenny *soirée*.' This roused Campbell's democratic blood, and he immediately offered to fill the breach. 'Delta' proposed his health, and the audience got their hearts out by singing 'Ye Mariners of England.' Before the year ended he had again changed his residence. This time it was to 'spacious chambers' in Lincoln's Inn Fields, which, ignoring all the teachings of experience, he furnished so expensively that he had to undertake a new piece of hack work to cover the cost. The account of his difficulty with an Irish charwoman who sought to help him in arranging his books is at once amusing and pathetic. She understood, he says, neither Greek nor Latin, so that when he ordered her to bring such and such a volume of Athenæus or Fabricius she could only grunt like one of her native pigs. What did Campbell expect? Redding has a dreary picture of the disorder in which he found him one afternoon shortly after this. The rooms were in a state of extraordinary confusion. The breakfast things were still on the table, a coat was on one chair and a dressing-gown on another; pyramids of books were heaped on the floor, and papers lay scattered about in endless disarray. It was indeed a sad change from the neatness which had prevailed in Mrs Campbell's time.

About this date the illustrated edition of his poems was published, and he found himself in some perplexity over the disposal of the drawings, for which he had paid Turner £550. He had been assured that Turner's drawings were like banknotes, which would always bring their original price, but when he offered them for £300 no one would look at them, and Turner himself subsequently bought them for two hundred guineas. Of this illustrated edition two thousand five hundred copies went off within a twelvemonth; while of an edition on shorter paper the same number was sold in eleven months in Scotland alone. Those were happy days for poets!

At the close of this year (1837) the *Scenic Annual* appeared, containing four pieces of Campbell's own, notably his 'Cora Linn, or The Falls of Clyde,' which he had written while in Glasgow the previous summer. Evidently he had some doubts about the dignity of accepting the editorship of this work, which was issued by Colburn merely to use up some old plates. 'You will hear me much abused,' he says, 'but as I get £200 for writing a sheet or two of paper it will take a deal of abuse to mount up to that sum.' One cannot help recalling how Scott scorned to write for the *Keepsake*, but Scott's ideas of self-respect were very different from those of Campbell. In January 1838 Campbell intimates that he is busy on a popular edition of Shakespeare for Moxon. Needless to say, it was a good-for-nothing production. It is, however, a point in his favour that he had the grace to be ashamed of it. He said he had done it hurriedly, though with the right feeling. 'What a glorious fellow Shakespeare must have been!' he exclaimed, when talking about the book. 'Walter Scott was fine, but had a worldly twist. Shakespeare must have been just the man to live with.' This hint at Scott's worldliness is sufficiently amusing, to say the least, in view of Campbell's own sordid ambitions.

On the 10th of March he tells how he has been corresponding with the Queen. He had got his poems and his 'Letters from the South' bound with as much gilt as would have covered the Lord Mayor's coach—the bill was £6—and having sent the volumes to Windsor, they were, as such things always are, 'graciously accepted.' For an avowed democrat Campbell made an unaccountable outcry about this 'honour,' which produced nothing more substantial than an autograph portrait of Her Majesty. In truth, with all his good sense, he could be very foolish on occasion. He was one of the spectators at the coronation of the Queen in Westminster Abbey this year— later on he was presented at Court by the Duke of Argyll—and he declares that she conducted herself so well during the long and fatiguing ceremony, that he 'shed tears many times.' Why anyone should shed tears because a royal lady behaves herself becomingly would have been a puzzle for Lord Dundreary. But Campbell was given to blubbering on every conceivable and inconceivable pretext. Once when he went to visit Mrs Siddons he was 'overcome, even to tears, by the whole meeting'; and we hear of him crying like a child when drawing up some papers on behalf of the despoiled Poles. What tears are 'manly, sir, manly,' as Fred Bayham has it, may sometimes be difficult to decide, but there can be no question about the unmanly character of much of Campbell's snivelling.

In July he paid another visit to Scotland, this time in connection with family affairs. Mrs Dugald Stewart died while he was in Edinburgh, and one more link binding him to the past was broken. Returning to his lonely chambers, he reports himself as working from six in the morning till midnight, a treadmill business which he unblushingly admits to be due to sheer avarice. 'The money! the money!' he exclaims; 'the thought of parting with it is *unthinkable*, and pounds sterling are to me "dear as the ruddy drops that warm my heart."' He calls himself spendthrift—as wretched and regular a miser as ever kept money in an old stocking; and finds an excuse for himself only in the fact that he is getting more interested in public charities. His principal literary work was now a Life of Petrarch. Archdeacon Coxe had left a biography uncompleted, and Campbell agreed to finish it for £200. He found it, however, so stupid that he decided to write a Life of Petrarch himself, though he frankly allowed that until quite recently he had something like an aversion to Petrarch because of the monotony of his amatory sonnets, and his wild, semi-insane passion for Laura. He had nothing but pity for a man who could be in love for twenty years with a woman who was a wife and a prolific mother to boot. The Life of Petrarch occupied him until the spring of 1840. It was a sorry performance, and may be dismissed without further remark. Campbell had neither the sympathy with the Italian poet nor the intimate knowledge of his life and work which were requisite in his biographer, and the book is simply what he called it himself—a mere piece of manufacture.

Very little of importance had happened while he was engaged on this production. There were visits to Brighton and to Ramsgate in search of health; and another link had been severed by the death of Alison, his 'mind's father.' He had projected a small edition of his poems as a resource for his closing years, and in November 1839 Moxon had thrown off ten thousand copies in double column, to be sold at two shillings each. Of original lyrical work nothing of any note was produced, the pieces including 'My Child Sweetheart,' 'Moonlight,' and 'The Parrot.' In September 1840 he was at Chatham for the launch of a couple of warships, when he made a speech and wrote his lines on 'The Launch of a First-rate.' Campbell had a patriotic partiality for the navy, and liked to hear about the exploits of seamen, but his speech on this occasion was a great deal better than the verses which followed it.

Feeling more than ever the cheerlessness of his chambers, he now made another expensive change of residence. He longed for the comforts of a *home*, and with his niece, Margaret, the daughter of his deceased brother, Alexander Campbell, whom he brought from Glasgow to superintend his domestic arrangements, he leased the house No. 8 Victoria Square, Pimlico, about which he spoke to everybody as a child speaks about a new toy. He removed in the spring of 1841; but he had not been long in occupation when he fell ill and went off suddenly to Wiesbaden. Beattie says he would not abide strictly by regimen, and to his other complaints was now added an attack of rheumatism. At Wiesbaden he met Hallam, the historian, 'a most excellent man, of great acuteness and of immense research in reading,' but no other notability seems to have crossed his path. He benefited greatly by the waters and baths, and at Ems even managed to write the ballad of 'The Child and Hind,' the story of which, printed in a Wiesbaden paper, plagued him so that he could not help rhyming. This piece was obviously meant as an imitation of the old ballad, but it is as little successful as such imitations usually are.

Reaching London once more, he sat down contented—for the time being— at his own fireside; and in November he writes of his intention to live now as a gentleman poet. He was highly pleased with his niece. She was 'well-principled and amiable,' a 'nice, comfortable housekeeper,' and a 'tolerable musician.' Some people jeered at her for her scruples about going to the play, but Campbell allowed nothing to be said in her hearing that might alarm her pious feelings. He taught her French and Greek, engaged the best masters for her general education, and spared no expense in books. His affectionate feelings towards her are well expressed in the lines beginning 'Our friendship's not a stream to dry,' and a more tangible token of his regard was shown at his death, when he left her nearly the whole of his property.

He had now been busy for some time with 'The Pilgrim of Glencoe,' and the poem was published, with other short pieces, in February 1842. It fell still-born from the press. Some zealous admirer said it ought to have been as good as a bill at sight, but alack! the bill was found to be unnegotiable. The publisher made strenuous exertions to obtain a hearing for the poem, but all to no purpose. The public would not be roused from their indifference, and 'The Pilgrim of Glencoe' sunk at once into the shades of oblivion.

Campbell was manifestly unprepared for such a reverse. He had expected a quick and profitable return from the book, and had entered into heavy responsibilities, which now threatened his independence. One cannot help remarking again upon the mystery of these continued money difficulties. There was no reason why Campbell should be everlastingly in financial straits. He had his pension, he had been uncommonly lucky in the matter of legacies, he enjoyed property to the extent of £200 a year, and the profits of his work besides. There ought now to have been less cause than ever for pleading poverty. That there were difficulties is, however, abundantly evident, from the fact that he precipitately resolved to dispose of his house and retire to some retreat where he could live cheaply and await the advances of old age. London, he protested, was no longer the place for him. His friends, too, observed that his constitution was visibly failing: he walked with a feeble step, and his face wore an expression of languor and anxiety.

Under these disquieting conditions he made his will, and began to look about for the 'remote corner.' In the meantime he was preparing still another edition of his collected poems, which he intended to publish by subscription. He says that for several years past the sale of his books had been steadily going down, so that his poems, which had yielded him on an average £500 per annum, would not now bring him much more than a tenth of that amount. By keeping the book in his own hands he expected to make a goodly sum. But the experiment failed. The subscriptions dribbled in only at rare intervals, and some money having come to him from the death of his eldest and only surviving sister in March 1843, as well as a little legacy from Mr A'Becket, the new edition, like its predecessors, passed into the hands of Mr Moxon. The volume was a handsome one of four hundred pages, with fifty-six vignettes by leading artists. It had a not inconsiderable sale, and brought a substantial addition to Campbell's exchequer.

Unhappily he had neither health nor spirits to enjoy his improved fortunes. He had outlived all his own family; he was getting more and more depressed, more and more feeble. To leave London seemed ill-advised, but he was determined upon it, and having made excursions to Brittany and elsewhere in search of a place of retirement, he at length fixed on Boulogne.[3] There he arrived with his niece in July 1843. Redding saw him just before leaving and found him in good humour, though he appeared weak and looked far older than he was. He had sold a thousand volumes from his library, and injudiciously spent £500 on the purchase of an annuity, because he dreaded that he might run through the principal. Boulogne proved not uncongenial to his tastes—a gay place with many public amusements, the Opera and the 'Comedie,' as well as concerts and races. But he was never able to derive any pleasure from it. Even the books he had brought from London were never placed on their shelves.

He had still some work which he intended doing, particularly a treatise on ancient geography, but 'incurable indolence' overcame him, and he resigned himself to the arm-chair. He complained of weakness, and felt a gradually increasing disinclination for any kind of exertion. In March 1844 Beattie received from him the last letter he ever wrote. A rapid decay of bodily strength had set in, and he never rallied. He had frequently told Beattie, his 'kind, dear physician,' that if he ever fell seriously ill care should be taken to acquaint him with the fact. Beattie was accordingly summoned to Boulogne, but his services were unavailing, except in so far as he could make the closing days easier for the patient. When the end came, on the 15th of June, it came peacefully, so peacefully that those who were watching by the bedside hardly knew when the spirit had fled.

Thus died Thomas Campbell, the last of all his long family, 'a lonely hermit in the vale of years.' There was a story that a representative of the Glasgow Cemetery Company had waited on the poor enfeebled poet about a year before his death to beg his body for their new cemetery. However this may have been—and one would prefer not to believe the story—when Campbell wrote his 'Field Flowers' it seems clear that he contemplated a grave by the Clyde. Redding says: 'He often spoke of our going down together to visit the scenery, and of his preference for it as a last resting-place.' But the field-flowers, 'earth's cultur'less buds,' were not to bloom on his grave. His body was brought to England, and on the 3rd of July was laid with great pomp in the Poets' Corner of Westminster Abbey, where a fine statue now marks his tomb. A deputation of Poles attended, and as the coffin was lowered a handful of earth from the grave of Kosciusko was scattered over the lid. It was a simple but touching tribute. Two points struck his intimate friends when they read the inscription on the coffin lid. He was described as LL.D., a distinction he detested, and as 'Author of "The Pleasures of Hope,"' which he detested too.

CHAPTER IX
PERSONAL CHARACTERISTICS AND PLACE AS A POET

Something of Campbell's person and character will have already been gathered from the foregoing pages. His friends unite in praise of his eyes and his generally handsome appearance as a young man. Lockhart says that the eyes had a dark mixture of fire and softness which Lawrence's pencil alone could reproduce. Patmore speaks of his 'oval, perfectly regular' features, to which his eyes and his bland smile gave an expression such as the moonlight gives to a summer landscape. The thinness of the lips is commented upon by several writers; and it is even said that Chantrey declined to execute a bust because the mouth could never look well in marble. Gilfillan observes that there was nothing false about him but his hair: 'he wore a wig, and his whiskers were dyed'—to match the wig! Most of his acquaintances remark on the wig, which in his palmy days was 'true to the last curl of studious perfection'; Lockhart alone declares that it impaired his appearance because his choice of colour was abominable. Byron's picture of him as he appeared at Holland House in 1813 has often been quoted: 'Campbell looks well, seems pleased and dressed to sprucery. A blue coat becomes him; so does his new wig. He really looked as if Apollo had sent him a birthday suit or a wedding garment, and was witty and lively.'

But the completest and most consistent description is to be found in Leigh Hunt's Autobiography. Hunt says: 'His skull was sharply cut and fine, with plenty, according to the phrenologists, both of the reflective and amative organs... His face and person were rather of a small scale; his features regular, his eye lively and penetrating; and when he spoke dimples played about his mouth, which, nevertheless, had something restrained and close in it. Some gentle puritan strain seemed to have crossed the breed and to have left a stamp on his face, such as we often see in the female Scotch face rather than on the male.' After Mrs Campbell's death in 1828 he lost something of his old finical neatness, but he continued to the last to be 'curious in waistcoats and buttons.' Madden speaks of him in his later years as 'an elderly gentleman in a curly wig, with a blue coat and brass buttons, very like an ancient mariner out of uniform and his natural element.' Before he left London for Boulogne, he would be seen in the streets with an umbrella tucked under his arm, his boots and trousers all dust and dirt, 'a perfect picture of mental and bodily imbecility.'

The best portrait of Campbell is the well-known one by Sir Thomas Lawrence, engraved in most editions of his works. It was painted when he was about forty years of age, and represents him very much as Byron described him. Redding, who had good means of judging, says that, barring the lips, which were too thick, it was 'the perfection of resemblance.'

Campbell was somewhat vain of his appearance, and would never have asked, like Cromwell, to be painted warts and all. He had, in particular, a sort of feminine objection to an artist making him look old. Late in life he sat to Park, the sculptor, when his desire to be reproduced *en beau* made him decline to take off his wig. Park made a very successful bust, but Campbell disliked it just because of its extreme truthfulness. In the Westminster Abbey statue by Marshall, the features, according to those who knew him, are preserved with happy fidelity, though the attitude is somewhat theatrical, and we get the notion of a much taller and more athletic figure.

Campbell's social habits have been variously described. There can be no doubt that occasionally he took too much wine; so did most people at that time. Beattie makes a long story about it, pleading this and that in extenuation, but there is no need to enlarge on the matter now. It was merely, as Campbell said himself, a case of being unable to resist 'such good fellows.' He was never a solitary drinker, like De Quincey with his opium. When he was left a widower he went more into company than he had done before; and apart from his special temptations, there was the fact that with his excitable temperament his last defences were carried before a colder man's outworks. Moreover, he found that wine gave an edge to his wit, and hence he may often have passed the conventional bounds in the mere endeavour to promote the hilarity of his friends.

His other indulgences seem to have been quite innocent. Hunt hints at his love of a good dinner, which indeed has been seen from his letters. He was almost as fond of the pipe as Tennyson, and he had even been known to chew tobacco when he found it inconvenient to smoke. He liked music, though he knew no more about the theory of the art than Scott. The national songs of his country specially appealed to him; and he was severe upon Dr Burney, the musical historian, because he had not done justice to the old English composers. He played the flute—how wonderfully flute-playing has gone out of fashion!—and could 'strike in now and then with a solo.' His early 'vain little weak passion' to have 'a fine characteristic, manly voice' was never realised, but with such voice as he had, he often gratified his friends in a Scots song or in his own 'Exile of Erin.' 'The Marseillaise' was his favourite air, and when on his deathbed he several times asked his niece to play it.

But Campbell gave himself very little time for recreation and social enjoyment. Most of his waking hours were spent in his study, where he dawdled unconscionably over the lightest of tasks. As a rule he attempted verse only when in the mood. He told George Thomson, who had asked him for some lyrics, that if he sat on purpose to write a song he felt sure it would be a failure. On the other hand, he sat down to produce prose with the clockwork regularity of Anthony Trollope. He wrote very slowly, and would often recast a whole piece out of sheer caprice, the second version being not seldom inferior to the first. Several of his friends speak of his practice of adding pencil lines to unruled paper for making transcripts of his verse. His habits of study were erratic and desultory. He could not fix his thoughts for any length of time; yet he always pretended to be prodigiously busy. Even the minutes necessary for shaving he grudged: a man, he said, might learn a language in the time given to the razor. Scott wondered that he did so little considering the number of years he devoted to literature. But the reason is plain: he did not know how to economise his time. His imagination was active enough, but it was ill-regulated and flighty, and his incapacity for protracted exertion led to the abandonment of many well-conceived designs. This instability, this restless, wayward irresolution, was the weak point in his character. He would start of a sudden into the country in order to be alone, and he would be back in London next day. He would arrange visits in eager anticipation of enjoyment, and when he arrived at his destination would ask to be immediately recalled on urgent editorial business! 'There is something about me,' he truly said, 'that lacks strength in brushing against the world, and battling out the evil day.' And he was right when he named himself 'procrastination Tom.'

Campbell was not, in the usual sense of the term, a society man. He liked the company of ladies, especially when they were pretty, but 'talking women' he detested. Even Madame de Staël he disparaged because she was fond of showing off. For the 'high gentry,' to use his own words, he had an 'unconquerable aversion.' To retain their acquaintance, he said, meant a life of idleness, dressing, and attendance on their parties. He censured his own countrymen for their snobbish deference to the great, citing an instance of Scott having become painfully obsequious in a company when some unknown lordling arrived. Anything like formality, above all the idea of being invited out for other than a social and friendly object, made him silent and even morose. 'They asked me to show me,' he observed of a certain function; 'I will never dine there again.' Lockhart, writing of this phase of his character, says there was no reason why he should not have been attentive to persons vastly his superiors who had any sort of claim upon him; no reason why he should not have enjoyed, and profited largely by enjoying, 'the calm contemplation of that grand spectacle denominated the upper world.' As a society star, Lockhart is perhaps to be excused for not sympathising with the position. Campbell had his bread to make by his own industry, and he could not possibly fill his hours with forenoon calls and nightly levees. But more than that, he was not formed, either by habit or by mode of thinking, for the conventional round of social life. A man who puts his knife in the salt-cellar—as, according to Lady Morgan, Campbell once did at an aristocratic table—is not made for associating with the 'high gentry.' The 'upper world' may indeed be, as Lockhart says it is, 'the best of theatres, the acting incomparably the first, the actresses the prettiest.' But Campbell seems always to have felt as much out of place there as a country cousin would feel in a greenroom. Various references in his letters suggest that he was troubled with a nervous self-consciousness, the bourgeois suspicion that his 'betters' were laughing in their sleeve at him, and the natural result was *gaucherie* and sometimes incivility. But among his equals he was another man. Hunt tells of one great day at Sydenham—a specimen, no doubt, of many such days— when Theodore Hook came to dinner and amused the company with some extempore drollery about a piece of village gossip in which Campbell and a certain lady were concerned. Campbell enjoyed the fun immensely, and 'having drunk a little more wine than usual,' he suddenly took off his wig and dashed it at Hook's head, exclaiming: 'You dog! I'll throw my laurels at you.' Little wonder that one who thus mingled vanity with horse-play was not quite at home among duchesses!

No two authorities agree as to Campbell's powers as a talker, but the truth would seem to be that he shone only at his own table or among his intimates, and even then, as already hinted, only when stimulated by wine. He was indeed too reserved to be quite successful as a conversationalist. One of his friends said he knew a great deal but was seldom in the mood to tell what he knew. He 'trifled in his table-talk, and you might sound him about his contemporaries to very little purpose.' As early as the year 1800 he remarked that he would always hide his emotions and personal feelings from the world at large, and although we come upon an occasional burst of confidence in his letters, he may be said to have kept up his reserve to the end. Madden called him 'a most *shivery* person' in the presence of strangers; Tennyson said he was a very brilliant talker in a *tête-a-tête*. According to an American admirer, he was quite commonplace unless when excited; Lockhart found him witty only when he had taken wine. Lytton was disappointed with him on such occasions as he met him in general society, but spoke of an evening at his house when Campbell led the conversation with the most sparkling talk he had ever heard. Nothing, he said, could equal 'the riotous affluence of wit, of humour, of fancy' that Campbell poured forth.

To this may be added a second quotation from Leigh Hunt, which will serve to bring out some other points. Hunt writes:

Those who knew Mr Campbell only as the author of 'Gertrude of Wyoming' and 'The Pleasures of Hope' would not have suspected him to be a merry companion overflowing with humour and anecdote, and anything but fastidious. Those Scotch poets have always something in reserve … I know but of one fault he had, besides an extreme cautiousness in his writings, and that one was national—a matter of words, and amply overpaid by a stream of conversation, lively, piquant, and liberal, not the less interesting for occasionally betraying an intimacy with pain, and for a high and somewhat overstrained tone of voice, like a man speaking with suspended breath, and in the habit of subduing his feelings. No man felt more kindly towards his fellow-creatures, or took less credit for it. When he indulged in doubt and sarcasm, and spoke contemptuously of things in general, he did it, partly, no doubt, out of actual dissatisfaction, but more perhaps than he suspected out of a fear of being thought weak and sensitive; which is a blind that the best men commonly practise. He professed to be hopeless and sarcastic, and took pains all the while to set up a University.

He seems to have had a very good opinion of his own powers as a talker, and apparently he sometimes failed from sheer over-anxiety to shine. At Holland House he used to set himself up against Sydney Smith. Of one visit he says: 'I was determined I should make as many good jokes and speak as much as himself; and so I did, for though I was dressed at the dinner-table much like a barber's clerk, I arrogated greatly, talked quizzically, metaphorically. Sydney said a few good things; I said many.'

This is, of course, all flummery, whether Campbell was really serious in his assertion or not. Whatever wit he may have shown on rare occasions, he was not, like Sydney Smith, naturally witty. As a writer his *forte* lay in the didactic and rhetorical, and when he attempted to move in a lighter step he became ridiculous. 'There never was a man,' says Redding, 'who had less of the comic in his character than Campbell.' Some of his friends aver that he often had fits of punning, but such of his puns as have survived do not lead us to believe that he can ever have been very successful in that most mechanical form of wit. 'I have only one muse and you two, so you must be the better poet,' he once said to Redding; the explanation being that Campbell's house had one mews while Redding's house had two. At another time Redding having complained that he could not get into his desk for his cash because he had lost the key, Campbell replied: 'Never mind, if nothing better turns up you are sure of a post among the *lack-keys*.' When Hazlitt published 'The New Pygmalion' he declared that the title ought to have been 'Hogmalion'; and he told a friend that the East was the place to write books on chronology because it was the country of *dates*. These are specimens of Campbell's puns, from which it will be gathered that humour was certainly not one of his endowments.

Nowhere does this lack of real humour come out more clearly than in his letters, which are plain and ponderous almost to the verge of boredom. There is nothing in them of that ever-glowing necessity of brain and blood which makes the letters of Scott and Byron, for example, so humanly interesting. He has no lightness like Walpole, no quiet whimsicality like Cowper, no sidelights on literature and life like Stevenson. Lockhart's apology for him is that, chained so fast to the dreary tasks of compilation, he could not be expected to have a stock of pleasantry for a copious correspondence. But none of the brilliant letter-writers can be suspected of having kept a choice vintage of epistolary Falernian in carefully sealed bottles. A man's individuality expresses itself in his letters as naturally as a fountain flows. The truth is that Campbell was too reserved, or too artificial, or both, to make a good letter-writer.

By all accounts he had not the best of tempers; indeed he admitted that to many people he had been 'irritable, petulant, and overbearing.' Of personal quarrels, however, he had very few; and although he said that he had been several times on the point of sending challenges, he was not once concerned in a duel. His chivalry led him to take the then bold step of defending Lady Byron's character against the strictures of her husband, and when the press abused him he regarded it as a compliment. Of his kind-heartedness there are many proofs, apart from the generous way in which he dealt with his widowed mother and his sisters. No man was more ready to perform a good deed. His charities were varied and widespread. He held the view that in tales of distress one can never believe too much, and naturally he was often imposed upon. When he was in the country he seldom wrote without some confidential communication in the way of largess, often in a pecuniary form. On one occasion he sent Redding a couple of pounds for a poor unfortunate whom he had been trying to reclaim. He made strenuous efforts to get the child of a couple who had been condemned to death adopted by some kindly person; and there is a story of him weeding out hundreds of volumes from his library to help a penniless widow to stock a little book shop. When subscriptions were being asked for a memorial to Lord Holland, he excused himself by saying that he must give all he could spare to the Mendicity Society.

At the same time, in money matters he was almost criminally careless. The British Consul at Algiers said that his servant might have cheated him to any extent. He disliked making calculations of cash received or paid away, and there were times when he knew nothing of the real state of his finances. He would profess to be in great distress about money when, as a matter of fact, he had a roll of bank notes in his pocket. In 1841 Beattie, while he was absent at Wiesbaden, found in an old slipper at the bottom of a cupboard in his house a large number of notes twisted into the form of 'white paper matches.' When reproached with this piece of imprudence Campbell, admitting that the security was 'slippery,' remarked that 'it must have happened after putting on my night-cap.' At certain periods of his life, notably after his wife's death, he was positively miserly, but even then he had his wayward fits of generosity. He would throw away pounds one day, and the next day grudge sixpences. Very often he forgot what he had spent or given in charity, but he never forgot what he owed.

One of the most charming traits in his character was his love for children. As he put it in his 'Child Sweetheart,' he held it a religious duty

To love and worship children's beauty.

They've least the taint of earthly clod—

They're freshest from the hand of God.

He could not bear to see a child crossed, to hear it cry, or have it kept reluctantly to books. Once at St Leonards he drew a little crowd around him on the street while trying to soothe a sick baby. What he called 'infantile female beauty' especially attracted him: '*he*-children,' he said, not very elegantly, 'are never in beauty to be compared with *she* ones.' He saw a remarkably pretty little girl in the Park, and was afterwards so haunted by the vision that he actually inserted an advertisement in the *Morning Chronicle* with the view of making her acquaintance. Hoaxes were the natural result. One reply directed him to the house of an old maid—'a wretch who,' as he used to say with peevish humour, 'had never heard of either me or my poetry.' Campbell was a man of sixty when this incident occurred. His friends not unreasonably suspected his sanity; but he was only putting into practice the theory which he propounded in the lines just quoted.

Politically Campbell was a Whig of the Whigs, with rancorous prejudices which sometimes led him into unpleasant scrapes. On the question of Freedom he held very pronounced opinions. He was called the bard of Hope, but he was the bard of Liberty too. He abhorred despotism of all kinds. 'Let us never think of outliving our liberty,' he once wrote. The emancipation of the negroes he termed 'a great and glorious measure.' He does not seem to have been a perfervid Scot, though he speaks of something offending his tartan nationality. We are told that he never spared the disadvantages of his country's climate, nor the foibles of the Lowlanders, whatever these may have been; but just as Johnson loved to gird at Garrick, though allowing no one else to censure him, so Campbell would not permit his native country to be attacked by another. He once rejected an otherwise suitable paper for the *New Monthly* because something which the writer had said about Edinburgh did not meet with his approval.

Of his religious views very little is to be learnt, certainly nothing from his poems. Beattie says that as a young man he suffered great anxiety on the subject of religion, and spent much time in its investigation before he arrived at 'satisfactory conclusions.' What these conclusions were does not exactly appear. Redding expressly affirms that he was sceptical, adding that he was very cautious in discussing religious subjects with strangers. His freedom from bigotry was generally remarked: he condemned every form of intolerance, and never cared to ask a man what his creed was. He told his nephew Robert, who seems to have had some misgivings on the point, that he could get no harm by attending a Roman Catholic Church. 'God listens to human prayers wherever they are offered up.' The Catholics might be mistaken, but persecution was not a necessary part of their system; and if it were, did not Calvin and the Kirk of Geneva, 'which is the mother of the Scotch Kirk,' get Servetus burnt alive for being a heretic? Campbell himself seldom went to church in London, but when he was in Scotland he did as the Scots did, and heroically sat out the sermon. It is clear that his countrymen, of whose rigid righteousness he had many good stories, did not regard him as heterodox, otherwise the General Assembly would never have asked him, as they did in 1808, to make a new metrical version of the Psalms 'for the benefit of the congregations.' Nor is it certain that he was really sceptical, though it is very likely that he hesitated upon some points of dogma. It is, however, only in his later years that we get any indication of his religious sensibility, and then only of the vaguest kind. When Mrs Campbell died he exclaimed, as if he had doubted the fact before, 'There *must* be a God; that is evident; there must be an all-powerful, inscrutable God.' Again, when speaking of the sufferings of the Poles, he remarked: 'There *is* a Supreme Judge, and in another world there will be rewards and punishments.' But we are not justified in forming any conclusion about his settled religious convictions from emotional outbursts resulting from special circumstances and in the shadow of the tomb. In all likelihood he paid the conventional observance to religion, and, if he thought about doctrines at all, took care not to shock his family and prejudice his popularity with any expression of heterodoxy.

Campbell's literary pasturage does not appear to have been very wide or very rich. Robert Carruthers, of Inverness, who wrote an interesting account of some mornings spent with him, says his library was not extensive. There were one or two good editions of the classics, a set of the 'Biographie Universelle,' some of the French, Italian, and German authors, the Edinburgh Encyclopædia, and several standard English works, none very modern. Apparently he made no attempt to keep abreast of current literature; he stuck by his old favourites, and would often be found poring over Homer or Euripides. In his early days Milton, Thomson, Gray, and Goldsmith were his idols among the poets. Goldsmith, it was said, he could never read without shedding tears, another instance of his tendency to snivel. Thomson's 'Castle of Indolence' is frequently mentioned with approbation in his letters—'it is a glorious poem,' he said to Carruthers—and seems, indeed, to have been to some extent the model of his 'Gertrude.' Allan Ramsay he called one of his prime favourites, but, strange to say, he does not appear to have regarded Burns with any special enthusiasm. Certainly he told the poet's son that Burns was the Shakespeare of Scotland, and 'Tam-o'-Shanter' a masterpiece;

but, on the other hand, he contended—unaccountably enough, for surely Burns' nationality was the very fount of his inspiration—that Burns was 'the most un-Scotsman-like Scotsman that ever existed'; and in conversation he was known to have denounced his own countrymen for their extravagant adulation of the Ayrshire poet.

Campbell had something of Southey's amiable weakness for minor bards, and would often praise work which he must have known to be of poor quality. He thought very highly of James Montgomery of Sheffield; and he once called Mrs Hemans 'the most elegant poetess that England has produced.' He had no great admiration for the Lake School of poets. He declared that while doing some good in freeing writers from profitless and custom-ridden rules, they went too far by substituting licentiousness for wholesome freedom. For Coleridge's poetry he evinced an especial distaste, due partly, no doubt, to the fact that Coleridge had attacked 'The Pleasures of Hope' in his lectures. Of his criticism he spoke more favourably, but maintained that he had borrowed many of his ideas from Schlegel. In French poetry his favourite was Racine, whose tenderness, he said, was unequalled even by Shakespeare. But perhaps of all the poets his darling was Pope, whom he defended in a manner described by Byron as 'glorious.' The 'Rape of the Lock' he held to be unsurpassed. Of three American writers— Channing, Irving and Bryant—he had the highest opinion. The first he considered 'superior as a prose writer to every other living author,' a statement at which we can only raise our eyebrows. Among the novelists he specially extolled Smollett and Fielding. To the latter he says he never did justice in his youth, but shortly before his death he wrote that he had come to 'venerate' him, and to regard him as the better philosopher of the two, the truer painter of life. All this shows no exceptional critical discernment; and Sydney Smith was no less happy in his phrase than usual when he said that Campbell's mind had 'rolled over' a large field. A rolling stone gathers no moss. But that is more than Smith could have meant.

And now what, it must be asked, is Campbell's place as a poet? Before trying to answer the question it is necessary to understand exactly what we mean by it. If a poet's place depends on the extent to which he is read, then Campbell has no place, or almost none. He is not read, save by school-children for examinations. Milton and many another, it might be said, are in the same case; but there is a difference. Milton will always remain a supreme model, or at least a suggestive fount of inspiration; and the lover of poetry can be sure of never turning to him without some pleasure, some gain. But Campbell's pages are not turned to by the lover of poetry for solace or refreshment, for inspiration or guidance. As Horace Walpole said of two poems by writers to whom Campbell owed something—Akenside and Thomson—'the age has done approving these poems, and has forgot them.' What is this but to say that the poems in the main are lacking in the one essential—the *poetic*? The well-spring of poetry was not vouchsafed to Campbell. He worked from the outside, not from the depths of his own spirit. He spoke of having a poem 'on the stocks,' of beating out a poem 'on the anvil.' By these words does he not stand, before the highest tribunal, condemned? We read of him polishing and polishing until what little of original idea there was must have been almost refined away. We never hear of him bringing forth his thoughts with pain and travail. His letters are full of complaints about his vein being dried up, of his mind being too much cumbered with mundane concerns to have leisure for poetry; but we never once get a hint of any real misgiving as to his powers. 'There is no greater sin,' said Keats, 'than to flatter oneself with the idea of being a great poet... How comfortable a thing it is to feel that such a crime must bring its own penalty, that if one be a self-deluder, accounts must be balanced!'

Time has brought in its revenges for Campbell. His poems enshrine no great thoughts, engender no consummate expression. Felicities, prettinesses, harmonies of a sort one may find; respectabilities, vigour, patriotic and liberal sentiments declaimed with gusto. But these do not raise him above the level of a third-rate poet. His war songs will keep him alive, and that after all is no mean praise.

FOOTNOTES

[1] It may be convenient to set down in a note a list of Campbell's brothers and sisters, with dates of birth and death. The details are from the family Bible: Mary, 1757-1843; Isabella, 1758-1837; Archibald, 1760-1830; Alexander, 1761-1826; John, 1763-1806; Elizabeth, 1765-1829; Daniel, 1767-1767; Robert, 1768-1807; James, 1770-1783; Daniel, 1773-? Archibald and Robert went to Virginia, and John to Demerara.

[2] As these sheets are passing through the press, Mr W. K. Leask reminds me of Aytoun's visit to the Scottish Monastery as recorded in the 'Lays of the Scottish Cavaliers.' And of course the reference in 'Redgauntlet' is well known.

[3] Since these lines were written, a memorial tablet has been placed on the house in the Rue St Jean where Campbell resided. The tablet describes him as 'the celebrated English poet.' Was he not, then, a Famous Scot?

www.ingramcontent.com/pod-product-compliance
Lightning Source LLC
Chambersburg PA
CBHW021947190326
41519CB00009B/1173